# First World War
and Army of Occupation
# War Diary
France, Belgium and Germany

15 DIVISION
44 Infantry Brigade
Seaforth Highlanders (Ross-shire Buffs, the Duke of Albany's)
8th Battalion
1 March 1916 - 31 July 1916

WO95/1939/2

The Naval & Military Press Ltd
www.nmarchive.com
**Published in association with The National Archives**

Published by

## The Naval & Military Press Ltd

Unit 10 Ridgewood Industrial Park,
Uckfield, East Sussex,
TN22 5QE England
Tel: +44 (0) 1825 749494

www.naval-military-press.com

www.nmarchive.com

*This diary has been reprinted in facsimile from the original. Any imperfections are inevitably reproduced and the quality may fall short of modern type and cartographic standards.*

© **Crown Copyright**
**Images reproduced by permission of The National Archives, London, England, 2015.**

# Contents

| Document type | Place/Title | Date From | Date To |
|---|---|---|---|
| Heading | War Diary Of 8th (S) Battn. Seaforth Highlanders. From 1st March 1916. To 31st March 1916. Lieut Col. 31st March 1916 Cmdg. 8th Seaforth Highlanders Vol 4 | | |
| War Diary | Rats 14 Bis Section | 01/03/1916 | 02/03/1916 |
| War Diary | Noeux-Les-Mines | 03/03/1916 | 08/03/1916 |
| War Diary | Hulluch Section | 09/03/1916 | 20/03/1916 |
| War Diary | Mazingarbe | 21/03/1916 | 25/03/1916 |
| War Diary | Allouagne | 25/03/1916 | 31/03/1916 |
| Heading | War Diary Of 8th (Sec) Battn. Seaforth Highlanders from 1st April 1916 to 30th April 1916 Lieut Col. 6th May 1916 Commanding 8th (Ser) Battn Seaforth Highlanders Vol 5 | | |
| War Diary | Allouagne | 01/04/1916 | 06/04/1916 |
| War Diary | Allouagne Flechin | 07/04/1916 | 07/04/1916 |
| War Diary | Flechin | 08/04/1916 | 09/04/1916 |
| War Diary | Allouagne | 10/04/1916 | 25/04/1916 |
| War Diary | Bethune | 26/04/1916 | 26/04/1916 |
| War Diary | Quarry Section Bde Support | 26/04/1916 | 29/04/1916 |
| War Diary | Quarry Section | 30/04/1916 | 30/04/1916 |
| Miscellaneous | Quarry Section Right Sub Section | 30/04/1916 | 30/04/1916 |
| Heading | War Diary Of 8th (Service) Battalion Seaforth Highlanders. From-1-5-1916. To-31-5-16. In The Field. 4-6-1916. Vol 6 | | |
| War Diary | Rt Sub Section Quarry Section. | 01/05/1916 | 02/05/1916 |
| War Diary | Pt. Sub Section | 03/05/1916 | 03/05/1916 |
| War Diary | Rt Sub Section Quarry Section. | 04/05/1916 | 04/05/1916 |
| War Diary | Brigade Reserve Quarry Section | 05/05/1916 | 06/05/1916 |
| War Diary | Brigade Reserve | 07/05/1916 | 08/05/1916 |
| War Diary | Rt. Sub Section Quarry Section | 09/05/1916 | 09/05/1916 |
| War Diary | Rt. Sub Section | 10/05/1916 | 10/05/1916 |
| War Diary | Rt. Sub. Section Quarry Section | 10/05/1916 | 11/05/1916 |
| War Diary | Bethune | 11/05/1916 | 11/05/1916 |
| War Diary | Sailly La Bourse | 12/05/1916 | 14/05/1916 |
| War Diary | Bethune | 14/05/1916 | 19/05/1916 |
| War Diary | Brigade Support Hohenzollern Section | 20/05/1916 | 22/05/1916 |
| War Diary | Hohenzollern Section | 23/05/1916 | 23/05/1916 |
| War Diary | Left Sub-Section Hohenzollern Section | 24/05/1916 | 31/05/1916 |
| Map | Right Battn From Appendix I | | |
| Miscellaneous | Operation Order By Lieut Colonel W.A. Thomson Comdg: 8th (Service) Bn. Seaforth Highlanders. Appendix 2 | | |
| Miscellaneous | Operation Order By Lt Colonel N.A. Thomson Comdg: 8th Bn. Seaforth Highlanders. 7th May 16 Appendix 3 | 07/05/1916 | 07/05/1916 |
| Miscellaneous | Operation Order By Major. G.M. Lumsden, Comdg: 8th Bn. Seaforth Highlanders. 9-5-1916. Appendix 4 | 09/05/1916 | 09/05/1916 |
| Miscellaneous | Operation Order By Major G.M. Lumsden. Comdg 8th Seaforth Hdrs Appendix 5 | 13/05/1916 | 13/05/1916 |
| Operation(al) Order(s) | Operation Order No. 1 By Major G.M. Lumsden. Comdg 6th (S) Bn. Seaforth Highlanders Appendix 6 | 18/05/1916 | 18/05/1916 |

| | | | |
|---|---|---|---|
| Miscellaneous | 8th Seaforth Hdrs D 535 O.C. All Companies Appendix 7 | 18/05/1916 | 18/05/1916 |
| Operation(al) Order(s) | Operation Order No. 2 By Lieut. Col. W.A. Thomson Commdg 8th (S) Battn Seaforth Highlanders. Appendix 8 | 22/05/1916 | 22/05/1916 |
| Map | Appendix 9 | | |
| Heading | 8th Seaforths Vol 3 15th Div | | |
| Heading | War Diary Of 8th (S) Battn Seaforth Highlanders From 1st June 1916 To 30th June 1916 Volume XII In The Field | | |
| War Diary | Left Sub Section Hohenzollern Section | 01/06/1916 | 04/06/1916 |
| War Diary | Labourse | 05/06/1916 | 12/06/1916 |
| War Diary | Rt Sub Section Hulluch Section | 12/06/1916 | 16/06/1916 |
| War Diary | Brigade Support Hulluch Section | 17/06/1916 | 19/06/1916 |
| War Diary | Left Sub Section Hulluch Section | 20/06/1916 | 28/06/1916 |
| War Diary | Sailly La Bourse | 29/06/1916 | 30/06/1916 |
| Operation(al) Order(s) | Operation Order No. 3 By Lt Colonel N.A. Thomson, Comdg; 8th Bn. Seaforth Highlanders, 3rd June,16. Appendix I | 03/06/1916 | 03/06/1916 |
| Operation(al) Order(s) | Operation Order No. 1 By Lieut Col N.A. Thomson, Comdg; 8th Bn. Seaforth Highlanders, 11 June, 1916. Appendix II | 11/06/1916 | 11/06/1916 |
| Operation(al) Order(s) | Operation Order No. 2 By Lieut Col N.A. Thomson, Comdg; 8th Bn. Seaforth Highrs, June, 1st 1916. Appendix III | 01/06/1916 | 01/06/1916 |
| Operation(al) Order(s) | Operation Order No. 3 By Lieut Col N.A. Thomson, Comdg; 8th (S) Battn Seaforth Highrs, June, 15th 1916. Appendix IV | 15/06/1916 | 15/06/1916 |
| Operation(al) Order(s) | Operation Order No. 4 By Lieut Col N.A. Thomson, Comdg; 8th (S) Battn Seaforth Highrs, June, 15th 1916. Appendix V | 19/06/1916 | 19/06/1916 |
| Map | Appendix VI | | |
| Operation(al) Order(s) | Operation-Order No.5. By Lieut. Col. N.A. Thomson. Commdg. 8th Battn. Seaforth Highrs Appendix VII | 19/06/1916 | 19/06/1916 |
| Operation(al) Order(s) | Operation-Order No.6. By Lieut. Col. N.A. Thomson. Commdg. 8th Battn. Seaforth Highrs Appendix VIII | 20/06/1916 | 20/06/1916 |
| Operation(al) Order(s) | Operation-Order No.7. By Lieut. Col. N.A. Thomson. Commdg. 8th (S) Bn. Seaforth Highrs Appendix IX | 22/06/1916 | 22/06/1916 |
| Miscellaneous | (1) O.C. Trench Mortar Batty. 8th Seaforth Hrs. Appendix X | 25/06/1916 | 25/06/1916 |
| Operation(al) Order(s) | Operation Order No. 8 By Lieut Col N.A. Thomson O.S.O. Commdg. 8th Bn. Seaforth Highrs Appendix XI | 25/06/1916 | 25/06/1916 |
| Miscellaneous | 44th Brigade B.M. /32 | 24/06/1916 | 24/06/1916 |
| Miscellaneous | Programme Of L.W's And Smoke. | 23/06/1916 | 23/06/1916 |
| Miscellaneous | Programme Of L.W's And Smoke. | 13/06/1916 | 13/06/1916 |
| Operation(al) Order(s) | 44th Infantry Brigade Operation Order No. 62. Appendix XII | 25/06/1916 | 25/06/1916 |
| Miscellaneous | All Recipients Of Operation Order No. 9 Dated 26th. June 1916. Appendix XIII | 26/06/1916 | 26/06/1916 |
| Operation(al) Order(s) | Operation-Order. No. 9. By Lieut. Col N.A. Thomson D.S.O. Commdg. 8th. Battn. Seaforth Highlanders. June 26th. 1916 | 26/06/1916 | 26/06/1916 |
| Heading | War Diary Of 8th(Service) Battalion Seaforth Highlanders From 1st July 1916 To 31st July 1916 (Volume 13) In The Field | | |
| War Diary | Sailly-La Bourse. | 01/07/1916 | 06/07/1916 |

| Type | Description | Date From | Date To |
|---|---|---|---|
| War Diary | Bde Support Hohenzollern Section. | 06/07/1916 | 08/07/1916 |
| War Diary | Bde Support Hohenzollern | 09/07/1916 | 09/07/1916 |
| War Diary | Bde Support Hohenzollern Section | 10/07/1916 | 11/07/1916 |
| War Diary | Left Sub Section Hohenzollern Section | 11/07/1916 | 22/07/1916 |
| War Diary | Noeux Les Mines | 22/07/1916 | 22/07/1916 |
| War Diary | Noeux Les Mines Ourton | 23/07/1916 | 23/07/1916 |
| War Diary | Ourton | 24/07/1916 | 26/07/1916 |
| War Diary | Aven Doignt | 27/07/1916 | 27/07/1916 |
| War Diary | Barly | 28/07/1916 | 28/07/1916 |
| War Diary | Gezaincourt | 29/07/1916 | 31/07/1916 |
| War Diary | Naours | 31/07/1916 | 31/07/1916 |
| Operation(al) Order(s) | Operation Order No. 1. By Lieut. Col. N.A. Thomson, D.S.O., Commanding 8th. Battalion Seaforth Highlanders | | |
| Miscellaneous | Defence-Scheme Left-Sub-Section-Hohenzollern Section | 11/07/1916 | 11/07/1916 |
| Map | | | |
| Miscellaneous | Appendix "C" Company. | | |
| Miscellaneous | Appendix IX "C" Company | | |
| Operation(al) Order(s) | Operation Order No. 3 By Lieut. Col. N.A. Thomson D.S.O. Commdg 8th Battn Seaforth Highrs. | | |
| Miscellaneous | Appendix. "C" Company. | | |
| Miscellaneous | Report On State Of Enemy Trenches From Information Gathered Diary Said On 10/11th July 1916. | 10/07/1916 | 10/07/1916 |
| Miscellaneous | Appendix "C" Company. | | |
| Miscellaneous | Appendix "B" Company | | |
| Miscellaneous | 8th. Battalion Seaforth Highlanders | 05/07/1916 | 05/07/1916 |
| Miscellaneous | 8th Seaforth Highlanders Defence Scheme Brigade Support Hohenzollern Section | 05/07/1916 | 05/07/1916 |
| Operation(al) Order(s) | Operation Order No. 2. By Lieut Col N.A. Thomson D.S.O. Comdg 8th Seaforth Highlanders | 10/07/1916 | 10/07/1916 |
| Miscellaneous | D 115. | 10/07/1916 | 10/07/1916 |
| Miscellaneous | Report On Operations In Left Sub-Section. Hohenzollern Section. | 10/07/1916 | 10/07/1916 |
| Miscellaneous | | | |
| Operation(al) Order(s) | Operation Order No.1. By Lieut. Colonel. N.A. Thomson., D.S.O. Comdg; 8th (Service) Battalion. Seaforth Highlanders. 9th July, 1916. | 09/07/1916 | 09/07/1916 |
| Map | | | |
| Map | Garrison Left Sub Section Ho Henzollern Section | | |
| Miscellaneous | Appendix Bomb Post And Grenade Stores | | |
| Miscellaneous | 8th Seaforth Highlanders D. 147 | 15/07/1916 | 15/07/1916 |
| Miscellaneous | To The Adjutant 8 Seaforth Highr. | 17/07/1916 | 17/07/1916 |
| Miscellaneous | C Form (Duplicate). Messages And Signals. | | |
| Miscellaneous | Intelligence Report To Noon | 19/07/1916 | 19/07/1916 |
| Miscellaneous | Tactical Progress Report By O.C. 8th Seaforth Highlander For 24 Hours ends 4 A.M. | 19/07/1916 | 19/07/1916 |
| Miscellaneous | Tactical Progress Report By O.C. 8th Seaforth Highlander For 24 Hours ends 12 A.M. | 20/07/1916 | 20/07/1916 |
| Miscellaneous | Tactical Progress Report By O.C. 8th Seaforth Highlander For 24 Hours ends 4 A.M. | 21/07/1916 | 21/07/1916 |
| Miscellaneous | All Recipients Of O.O. No. 4 Dated July 21st 1916 | 21/07/1916 | 21/07/1916 |
| Operation(al) Order(s) | Operation Order No. 4 By Lieut. Col N.A. Thomson D.S.O. Commdg 8th Battn Seaforth Highlanders | 21/07/1916 | 21/07/1916 |
| Operation(al) Order(s) | Operation Order No. 5 By Lieut. Col N.A. Thomson D.S.O. Commdg 8th Battn Seaforth Highlanders | 22/07/1916 | 22/07/1916 |

| | | | |
|---|---|---|---|
| Miscellaneous | March Table To accompany 44th Infantry Brigade Operation Order No. 67 | 22/07/1916 | 22/07/1916 |
| Miscellaneous | Headquarters Mass. | 24/07/1916 | 24/07/1916 |
| Miscellaneous | Head Quarters Huss | | |
| Operation(al) Order(s) | Operation Order No. 6 By Lieut. Col. N.A. Thomson, D.S.O. Commdg 8th (S) Battn. Seaforth Highlanders | 25/07/1916 | 25/07/1916 |
| Miscellaneous | March Table to accompany 44th Infantry Brigade Operation Order No.68 | 25/07/1916 | 25/07/1916 |
| Operation(al) Order(s) | Operation Order No 7 By Lieut. Col N.A. Thomson. D.S.O. Commdg. 8th (S) Battalion Seaforth Highlanders. | 26/07/1916 | 26/07/1916 |
| Miscellaneous | March Table to accompany 44th Infantry Brigade Operation Order No.69 | 26/07/1916 | 26/07/1916 |
| Operation(al) Order(s) | Operation Order No 8 By Lieut Col N.A. Thomson D.S.O. Commanding 8th Battn Seaforth Highlanders | 27/07/1916 | 27/07/1916 |
| Miscellaneous | All Recipients Of Operation Order No 8 Issued | 27/07/1916 | 27/07/1916 |
| Miscellaneous | Casualties For July 1916 | 00/07/1916 | 00/07/1916 |
| Miscellaneous | 44th Brigade B.M.667 | 31/07/1916 | 31/07/1916 |
| Miscellaneous | Of Officers Casualties July 1916 | | |
| Miscellaneous | March Table to accompany 44th Infantry Brigade Operation Order No. 70 | 30/07/1916 | 30/07/1916 |
| Miscellaneous | 44th Brigade B.M.648 15th Div. No.1393 G.S. | 29/07/1916 | 29/07/1916 |
| Operation(al) Order(s) | Operation Order No 9. By Lieut Col. N.A. Thomson D.S.O. Commdg. 8th (S) Battn. Seaforth Highrs. | 30/07/1916 | 30/07/1916 |
| Miscellaneous | Addressed Recipients Of 44th Brigade Operation Order No. 69. | 27/07/1916 | 27/07/1916 |
| Miscellaneous | March Table to accompany 44th Infantry Brigade B.M.635. | | |
| Miscellaneous | 44th Brigade B.M. 635. | 27/07/1916 | 27/07/1916 |
| Miscellaneous | | | |

8 Seaforths Vol 4

9.W/15 sheets

CONFIDENTIAL.

WAR. DIARY.

of

8th [S] BATTN. SEAFORTH. HIGHLANDERS.

FROM. 1st MARCH 1916.                    To 31st MARCH. 1916.


                                    Thomson
                                    LIEUT COL.

31st MARCH 1916.        CMDG. 8th SEAFORTH. HIGHLANDERS.

**Army Form C. 2118.**

# WAR DIARY
## or
## INTELLIGENCE SUMMARY.
*(Erase heading not required.)*

Instructions regarding War Diaries and Intelligence Summaries are contained in F. S. Regs., Part II. and the Staff Manual respectively. Title pages will be prepared in manuscript.

| Place | Date | Hour | Summary of Events and Information | Remarks and references to Appendices |
|---|---|---|---|---|
| Phils 14 Bis Section | 1/3/16 | | Bn in Brigade Support - The whole Battn were working on communication trenches leading to front line. (M.J.) | |
| " | 2/3/16 | | Bn in Brigade Support. At night the Battn were relieved by 7th K.O.S.B. - relief started at 7.30 p.m & was completed about 10.30 p.m. On relief the Battn moved into rest billets at MEUX LES MINES by main road via PHILOSOPHE & MAZINGARBE. (M.J.) | |
| Noeux-les-Mines | 3/3/16 | | Battn in Billets - The day was spent in general cleaning up of clothing, equipment. 2nd Lieut D.N. Cameron & 4 O.R. proceeded to Gosnay to undergo a course of instruction in Telescopic sights. (M.J.) | |
| Noeux-les-Mines | 4/3/16 | | Battn in Billets - Kit inspections by Company Officers - 2nd Lieut J.H. Ross & 16 O.R. commenced a Bayonet & Bombing Course at 44th Infe Bde Bombing School Noeux-les-Mines. The Divisional Baths were allotted to the Battn from 8 am - 8 p.m. All Companies had the use of the baths in turn. (M.J.) | |

Army Form C. 2118.

# WAR DIARY
## or
## INTELLIGENCE SUMMARY.
(Erase heading not required.)

Instructions regarding War Diaries and Intelligence Summaries are contained in F. S. Regs., Part II. and the Staff Manual respectively. Title pages will be prepared in manuscript.

| Place | Date | Hour | Summary of Events and Information | Remarks and references to Appendices |
|---|---|---|---|---|
| Noeux-les-Mines | 5/3/16 | | Battn in billets - Lieut-Col N.A. Thompson proceeded today to an Artillery Course at AIRE. Capt D.W.P. Strang assumed Command of the Battalion in Colonel Thompson's absence. Following working parties were found by the Battn - 2 officers & 100 O.R. under 216th A.T. Coy R.E. at Church Mazingarbe 8.30 a.m. — 1 officer & 75 men under 216th A.T. Coy R.E. at Church Mazingarbe at 8 a.m. — 6 officers & 300 men with 71st Field Coy R.E. | |
|  | | | " " " 9th " " " | |
|  | | | " " " 74th " " " | |
|  | | | at Cross Roads Philosophe at 6 p.m. | W.T. |
| Noeux-les-Mines | 6/3/16 | | Battn in billets - A draft of 1 officer (Lieut T.D.B. Macaulay) & 61 O.R. arrived from 15th Infantry Base Depot Etaples. With the exception of 9 O.R. the whole of this draft consisted of men who had belonged formerly to the 5th Battn Seaforth Highlanders, who had either been wounded or evacuated sick. — Owing to the inclemency of the weather no training was carried out but the day was spent in generally supervising & completing of kit re. fwd. | W.T. |

Army Form C. 2118.

# WAR DIARY
## or
## INTELLIGENCE SUMMARY.
(Erase heading not required.)

Instructions regarding War Diaries and Intelligence Summaries are contained in F. S. Regs., Part II. and the Staff Manual respectively. Title pages will be prepared in manuscript.

| Place | Date | Hour | Summary of Events and Information | Remarks and references to Appendices |
|---|---|---|---|---|
| Noeux-Les-Mines | 7/3/16 | | Battn in billets — The following working parties were found by the Battn — 1 officer & 50 O.R. under Divisional R.E. reports at FOSSE 3 PHILOSOPHE at 9am. 2 officers & 100 men under Divisional R.E. at PHILOSOPHE at 6pm. This party worked in trenches in HOLLOCH SECTION. A 2nd piper & drummer having joined with the draft on the 6th inst. the Band was 15 strong — Pipe-Major A. MacKenzie commanding & 6 pipers. | |
| Noeux-Les-Mines | 8/3/16 | | Battn in billets — At 4.45pm the Battn. marched out of NOEUX-LES-MINES to relieve the 8th Royal Scots in the right subsection of the HOLLOCH SECTION — 2 Coys ("B" & "C") 8th Seaforth Highrs were billets in PHILOSOPHE & 2 Coys ("A" & "D") 8th Inniskillings were attached to the Battn for instruction in trench warfare & proceeded to the trenches. "B" & "C" Coys 8th Seaforth Highrs remaining under the orders of the 8th Inniskillings — Companies were met by Guides at Level Crossing BULGOTTE at 5pm, proceeded from the Victoria Station to ASEN STATION thence by PISEN ALLEY to the trenches. The relief was completed by 9.30pm. The disposition of Companies was as follows, Left firing line "C" Coy 8th Inniskillings Right firing line "A" Coy 8th Sea Highrs Support line "D" Coy 8th Inniskillings. Reserve line "B" Coy 8th Sea Highrs. Kitbags, greatcoats, (school huts) are brought up in this subsection by 1st line transport to VICTORIA STATION & then pushed | |

# WAR DIARY
## or
## INTELLIGENCE SUMMARY.
(Erase heading not required.)

Army Form C. 2118.

Instructions regarding War Diaries and Intelligence Summaries are contained in F.S. Regs., Part II. and the Staff Manual respectively. Title pages will be prepared in manuscript.

| Place | Date | Hour | Summary of Events and Information | Remarks and references to Appendices |
|---|---|---|---|---|
| Hulluch Section | | | up by the French railway to POSEN STATION where ration parties provided by the Company in reserve meet them & take them to respective Companies. The Quartermasters Stores moved to MAZINGARBE. 1st Line transport remained at NOEUX-LES-MINES. LIEUT G.W. DUNCAN was left in charge of the Orderly Room at MAZINGARBE. | |
| | 9/3/16 | - | Tho' actually at rest - one of the quietest 24 hrs the Battn has spent in the trenches - Major G.M. LINDSAY, 9th Seaforth Highlanders joined for duty - LIEUT F.G. HART was granted authority to wear the badge of the rank of temporary Captain - LIEUT P.W. SPRAY RA attached as Observation in FLAMMEN [?] of observing | |
| " | 10/3/16 | - | Battn in trenches - no activity - Lieut Col M.A. THOMPSON returned from Artillery Course at AIRE & resumed command of the Battalion. | |
| " | 11/3/16 | - | Battn in trenches. The 8th Seaforth Highlanders 8th Companies 8th Munster [?]  were relieved by 9th Black Watch - On relief "A" Coy gt Seaforths & "C" & "D" Companies 8th Munster went moved back to billets in PHILOSOPHE & came under the Orders of 8th Munsters - "D" Company moved into Brigade Support in Tenth Avenue & "B" & "C" Coys moved up from billets in PHILOSOPHE to Tenth Avenue & rejoined the Battalion. "B" "C" & "D" Coys 9th Seaforth Highrs were therefore under the Orders of O/C 9th Seaforth Highrs. Return Yurth (a patrol has) no other troops up by French Railway from Victoria Mahra - Capt G.L. Andrew s/s ltt. proceeded to day | |

# WAR DIARY
## or
## INTELLIGENCE SUMMARY.
*(Erase heading not required.)*

Army Form C. 2118.

| Place | Date | Hour | Summary of Events and Information | Remarks and references to Appendices |
|---|---|---|---|---|
| HULLUCH SECTION | 11/3/16 | | On adjourns Grenade Class at 44th Inf/Bde Grenade School, Noeux-Les-Mines. | |
| HULLUCH SECTION | 12/3/16 | | Batln. in Brigade Support - Capt F.G. HART & 2/R. proceeded on a course in Lewis Gun & Lieut. W. MURRAY & 1/R. proceeded on a course in Vickers Gun. Both Courses at Divisional Machine Gun School. GOSNAY. Lieut. J. KEITH joined for duty from 10th Seaforth Highrs & was temporarily posted to "A" Coy. | |
| " | 13/3/16 | | Batln. in Brigade Support - The regular Machine Gun Section was relieved by the Reserve M/g Section - The relief the regular section moved into billets at PHILOSOPHE Kent R.T.W. Schofield was temporarily appointed Reserve Machine Gun Officer. A draft of 12 men arrived from 15th Inf Base Depot Etaples & were posted to Companies. | |
| " | 14/3/16 | | During this day the Battn. moved from Brigade Support to the Centre Subsection - HULLOCH Section - The Battn. relieved the 10th Gordon Highlanders - Two Companies Viz the 10th & 2 Companies 8th Innes/Killing attached - The Battn. occupied the Centre Subsection as follows. "A" Company left firing line - "B" Company right firing line - "C" Company in | |

T2134. Wt. W708—776. 500000. 4/15. Sir J. C. & S.

# WAR DIARY
## or
## INTELLIGENCE SUMMARY.
*(Erase heading not required.)*

Army Form C. 2118.

| Place | Date | Hour | Summary of Events and Information | Remarks and references to Appendices |
|---|---|---|---|---|
| Hulluch Section | 14/3/16 | | Support - "D" Company in Reserve. Battn. Headquarters moved to G.14.b.6.8. The frontage previously held by the Battn. extended from HAY ALLEY (inclusive) to VERDUN ALLEY (exclusive). On the relief of the Battn. by 7th Cameron Highlanders on the left "D" Company were to the right of the Battn. & 7th Cameron Highlanders on the left "D" Company relieved "K" Company 10th Gordon Highlanders at 7am. "A" Company left BRUAY & at 9am. proceeded by march from VERMELLES (LE RUTOIRE ALLEY) relieved "B" Company 8th Inniskillings. "C" Company relieved I Coy 10th Gordon Highlanders at Annequin. "B" Company relieved "A" Company 8th Inniskillings. "A" Company 8th Inniskillings Dr the relief of "B" Company 8th Inniskillings. "A" Company 8th Norfolks extended their line to take over "Southern Orp" this Orp lies at 6 to a Crater that had been blown in by Hell fire, the holding of the Orp had to be undertaken by "A" Company. Rations in this subsection are brought up by French Railway to POSH & ST. nt 7om. 25th O.R. were this day Sposes. wounded (inclunh 1045) | London Gazette Wednesday March 8th Hood 36C Edition 6 |
| | | 1.30 p.m. | Battn. in Cerks Subsection. Enemy were active with rifle grenades - 10 O.R. of "A" Company were wounded - work was carried on in general repair of trenches. 10.R. | |
| | 16/3/16 | | Battn. in Cerks Subsection. Enemy were this day Sposes. wounded. | |

# WAR DIARY
## or
## INTELLIGENCE SUMMARY
*(Erase heading not required.)*

Army Form C. 2118

| Place | Date | Hour | Summary of Events and Information | Remarks and references to Appendices |
|---|---|---|---|---|
| HOHENZOLLERN SECTION. | 16/3/16. | | occurred. The artillery covering our front had been put on reduced allowance of ammunition (144th Brigade B.A.S.I. dated 13 March) this was little affected, rendered by an artillery. Retaliation was the one organised with trench mortars & rifle grenades. | |
| HOHENZOLLERN SECTION. | 17/3/16. | | In the early morning the enemy made a small bombing attack on Lap 45 held by "B" Company 8th Beforts. This attack was repulsed, 10 grenades bombed the enemy opposite. Our casualties in this attack were 2 men wounded — 2 enemy casualties were also clearly observed shortly after this enemy were very active with rifle grenades. Capt J.J. Phyffe & 4 O.R. being wounded. [illegible crossed out] In the evening enemy were again active with rifle grenades & Lieut J Keith & Lieut Charncake & 3 O.R. were wounded & 1 man killed — 2 men of 9th Black Watch Machine Gun Section were also wounded in our cross-section. The successfully replied to enemy rifle grenade fire with French Batteries Calibre 3·7" Firs 3" Grenade fire with trench Mortars — 4½ light how. Battery calibre 9·30 & 9·2"m — About 100 rounds Enemy Artillery were this day active between 9.30 & 9.15 am — About 100 shells (of all calibres) came over our trenches — 3 direct hits being obtained on support trench — No casualties however. "D" Company were relieved at 4.30pm in Reserve trench by "D" Company 1st Cameron Highlanders during the [illegible] "D" Company P.H.E. & came under the orders of you relief moved into billets at PHILOSOPHE preceded today by a Bombing Course at 144 Cl. 9th Black Watch. — I.O.R. K.I.L.S. MINES. — This day Battn Headquarters moved to Bryan Bowery School. NCFOxx L.S.S. MINES. | |

# WAR DIARY
## or
## INTELLIGENCE SUMMARY
(Erase heading not required.)

Army Form C. 2118

| Place | Date | Hour | Summary of Events and Information | Remarks and references to Appendices |
|---|---|---|---|---|
| Hulluch Section | 17/3/16 | | The former headquarters of the Battn. in Brigade Support at G.17.d.8.8. | Trench Map 1/10000 36c. NW3 Sheet 6 |
| Hulluch Section | 18/3/16 | | Much enemy grenade activity - flights of 4 + 6 grenades coming over at a time. We replied again with hand mortars rifle grenades. No 2447/2 L.M. Battery (under 2nd Lieut H.D. Addis) fired 94 rounds. This battery was very successful in silencing the enemy took was carried on in Southern loop. The top was too exposed along the whole length of its Southern arm. 2 men of "A" Company were this day wounded. Enemy shelled PHILOSOPHE - VERMELLES very heavily between 5pm & 6.30pm. Owing to this shelling the transport which at this time was proceeding to VICTORIA Station with rations was held in MAZINGARBE for 1 hour. 2 men of "D" Company were wounded in PHILOSOPHE. It was afterwards discovered that at this hour the enemy had made an attack on the Division on our left (12th Division). | |
| Hulluch Section | 19/3/16 | | Enemy trench mortars active both rifle grenades & man "A". Coy killed & 3 men wounded. We again successfully silenced them with Trench Mortars. Hoppe Contl. Battalion Sharpshooter was this day killed in the support trench by a bullet. This man had done very successful work as a Sharpshooter. | |

# WAR DIARY or INTELLIGENCE SUMMARY

Army Form C. 2118

| Place | Date | Hour | Summary of Events and Information | Remarks and references to Appendices |
|---|---|---|---|---|
| Mazingarbe Section | 20/3/16 | | The Enemy were not so active this day. During the afternoon the Battn. are relieved by the 8th Battn. K.O.S.B. on relief moved by Lt. & Stores Alley & Tramelles to Billets at MAZINGARBE - "D" Company of the Cameron Highlanders reported its last at HOHEN-LES-MINES. "D" Company 8th Seaforths moved from PHILOSOPHE & proceeded to the Battalion at MAZINGARBE. - Capt. J. Murray & 10 O.R. proceeded on a course of instruction in Lewis Gun & Lieut D.B. Macaulay & 10 O.R. proceeded on a course of instruction in Vickers Gun. Both Courses were at Divisional Hd.Q. school GOSNAY. 2nd Lieut P. Roe & 4 O.R. joined this O.R. proceeded on a course to Divisional Base Depot & thereafter to Companies - A draft of 22 men O.R. joined this day from 15th (Infantry) Base Depot & thereafter to Companies - Capt. J.G. Hunt - Lieut J.S. Owens & 15 O.R. were granted leave to United Kingdom. [sd] | |
| MAZINGARBE | 21/3/16 | | The day was spent in general cleaning up & kit inspections by Company Commanders. The Regimental Baths were used by "A" & "B" Coys. [sd] | |
| MAZINGARBE | 22/3/16 | | Billets were inspected in the morning by Lt. Col. N.A. Thomson & Major G.M.Humeston. The Divisional Baths were allotted to the Battn. & were used by "C" & "D" Coys - "A" & "B" Coys had the use of the Regimental Baths. - 5 O.R. were reported missing to England & struck off the strength of the Battalion. [sd] | |

# WAR DIARY
## or
## INTELLIGENCE SUMMARY
(Erase heading not required.)

Army Form C. 2118

| Place | Date | Hour | Summary of Events and Information | Remarks and references to Appendices |
|---|---|---|---|---|
| MAZINGARBE | 23/3/16. | | Battn. in billets. Inspection of kits, arms, ammunition, gas helmets &c. — The following working parties were found by the Battn. (a) 2 officers 100 men "C" Coy — to work with 9th Gordons Highs (b) 2 officers 100 men "D" Coy — to work under 73rd Field Coy RE. (c) 1 officer 50 men "A" Coy to work under 9th Field Coy RE. 1 officer 50 men "B" Coy. These parties left MAZINGARBE at 6pm, 6.10pm & 6.20pm respectively these met by guides at cross roads PHILOSOPHE at 6.30pm. 3 officers NCO 3 O.R. were granted leave of absence to the United Kingdom. | |
| MAZINGARBE | 24/3/16. | | Battn. in billets. The Battn. was to have been inspected by the 1st Corps Commander but owing to the inclemency of the weather this inspection was cancelled. 30 O.R. were granted leave to UK. | |
| MAZINGARBE | 25/3/16. | | Battn. moved from MAZINGARBE to ALLOUAGNE & took over the same billets as they had occupied from Dec 15th to Jany 15th — "A" & "B" Companies together with 2 platoons of "C" Coy Signallers, Pioneers & Police left MAZINGARBE by platoons at two minutes interval at 8.15 am. & marched to NOEUX-LES-MINES where they entrained at 10.5 am. this party arrived at LILLERS at 11.15 am. & marched thence to ALLOUAGNE arriving there at 12.30 pm. This party was under Major G.M. Homsden. The remaining two platoons of "C" Coy & "D" Coy left MAZINGARBE by platoons at two minutes interval at 9 a.m. & marched to NOEUX-LES-MINES where they entrained at 10.45 am. the party which was under Capt C.C. | |

# WAR DIARY
## or
## INTELLIGENCE SUMMARY
(Erase heading not required.)

Army Form C. 2118.

| Place | Date | Hour | Summary of Events and Information | Remarks and references to Appendices |
|---|---|---|---|---|
| MUDPAGNE | 25/3/14 | | Forsyth arrived at LILLERS at 12 noon. Marching hence to ALLOUAGNE arriving here at 4.10pm. Follies transport moved from NOEUX-LES-MINES to ALLOUAGNE under Brigade Transport Officer. Lieut Mackenzie 10th Yorks via Vaudricourt, K4 central, Hersimmel, E25 a 6.6, D30 b 08. T/4 Cpl Quarles Les-Mines arrived at ALLOUAGNE at 12.15pm. 4 B.O.R. were granted leave to the United Kingdom. | Reference Map MINES Sheets 6 BETHUNE. |
| ALLOUAGNE | 26/3/14 | | Batten in billets - The Bath was again to have been inspected by 1st Corps Commander but owing to the inclemency of the weather this inspection was again cancelled. Divine Service was held at 10 a.m. in Divisional Recreation Room. Capt Robinson R.A.M.C. att'd Seaforth Hds was granted leave to United Kingdom during the absence his duties were taken over by Lieut O'Sullivan R.A.M.C. 4/5th Field Ambulance. 3 O.R. were also granted leave to United Kingdom. 2nd Lieut H.C. Duncan & 2 O.R. proceeded on a course of instruction in Physical Training & Bayonet fighting at CHENAY. | J.W. |
| ALLOUAGNE | 27/3/14 | | Batten in billets - Company Parades as follows:- 7 - 7.45 a.m. Physical Training & Saluting Drill. 10 - 12.30 p.m. Squad Drill - Musketry - Practice in the use of ICC. 3 p.m. - 4.30 p.m. Kit inspections & general fitting of equipment. 2nd Lieut L.A. Roland & 3 O.R. were granted leave of absence to United Kingdom. | |

2nd Lieut L.A. Roland & 3 O.R. were granted leave of absence to United Kingdom.

# WAR DIARY
## or
## INTELLIGENCE SUMMARY

(Erase heading not required.)

Army Form C. 2118.

| Place | Date | Hour | Summary of Events and Information | Remarks and references to Appendices |
|---|---|---|---|---|
| ALLOUAGNE | 28/3/16 | | Batt. in billets. Batt. to take part in an inspection of 44th Highland Brigade by General Sir Charles Munro Commanding 1st Army. The Brigade was drawn up on the Rake Squares in LILLERS in the formation of a hollow square — Honor guards were presented to an officer & Non Commissioned officers & men of Royal Engineers for gallantry in the field & after the awards had been given, the Brigade marched past General Munro & a. Mn. 7th Cantoons. 10th Gordons, 8th Seaforths, 9th Black Watch 8 O.R. were reported wounded to England & struck off the strength accordingly. | Apps |
| ALLOUAGNE | 29/3/16 | | Batt. in billets. Training was carried on by companies as on 27th inst. 1 Offr (2nd Lieut A.J.M.Mills) & 62 O.R joined the Battalion from the 3rd Batt. Seaforth Highlanders Cromarty. | (M) |
| HEUCHIN | 30/3/16 | | Batt. in billets. Platoon training under Company Arrangements. A Corporal & privates of 9th Gordon Highlanders (Pioneers) were attached to instruct in wire entanglements. 2nd Lieut W.M.Gardner joined for duty & was posted to "A" Company. Captain Sem. P. Henry was granted leave to United Kingdom — his duties were taken over by Lieut J.M. Duncan. Capt J.Y. Ryh & 5 O.R were reported wounded to England & struck off the strength accordingly. | |

# WAR DIARY
## or
## INTELLIGENCE SUMMARY

Army Form C. 2118.

| Place | Date | Hour | Summary of Events and Information | Remarks and references to Appendices |
|---|---|---|---|---|
| ALLOUAGNE | 3/3/16 | - | Batln in billets - The Batln had the use of the baths at AUCHEL & had all Companies had baths. 70 O.R. were reported involved to England & Struck off the Strength accordingly. (JM) | |

Seaforths Vol 5

CONFIDENTIAL

War Diary

of

8th (Ser) Battn. Seaforth Highlanders.

from 1st April 1916   to   30th April 1916.

6th May 1916.

J.H. Thomason
Lieut Col.
Commanding 8th (Ser) Battn Seaforth Highlanders

**Army Form C. 2118.**

# WAR DIARY
## or
## INTELLIGENCE SUMMARY
*(Erase heading not required.)*

Instructions regarding War Diaries and Intelligence Summaries are contained in F. S. Regs., Part II. and the Staff Manual respectively. Title Pages will be prepared in manuscript.

| Place | Date | Hour | Summary of Events and Information | Remarks and references to Appendices |
|---|---|---|---|---|
| ALLOUAGNE | 1/4/16 | — | Battn in billets — "A" "C" & "D" Coys took part in Battn Route March — Route - LOZINGHEM, AUCHEL, RAIMBERT, BURBURE, HAUT RIEUX, ALLOUAGNE. "B" Coy had the use of the Range on ALLOUAGNE-LAPUGNOY Road & 40 men of "B" Coy were also instructed in the construction of Wire Entanglements. | Reference Map HAZEBROUCK 5A. |
| ALLOUAGNE | 2/4/16 | — | Battn in billets — Church Parade at 9.30 a.m. in Divisional Recreation Room ALLOUAGNE. The draft of 62 O.R. which arrived on March 30th 1916 was inspected by Brigadier General Wilkinson Cmdg 144th Inf Bde. | Ind. |
| ALLOUAGNE | 3/4/16 | — | Battn in billets — Platoon Training under Company Arrangements including Gas Drill – handling of arms practice in the use of Smoke Helmets — 40 men of "C" Coy were instructed in the Construction of Wire Entanglements. | Ind. |
| ALLOUAGNE | 4/4/16 | — | Battn in billets — Company training — "A" & "B" practising "the Attack". "C" musketry on range. "D" Coy practice in construction of Wire entanglements. – Lieut. C. MacMillan & Lieut. J. Keith reported themselves to Bethune United Kingdom, were this day struck off the strength of the Battalion. | Ind. |
| ALLOUAGNE | 5/4/16 | — | Battn in billets. Company Training — "D" Company & "C" practice in construction of Wire entanglements — "A" Coy practice in construction of wire entanglements. — 3 O.R. reported sick & were died of wounds & 3 O.R. invalided to England were struck off the strength of Battalion accordingly. | Ind. |

Army Form C. 2118.

# WAR DIARY
# or
# INTELLIGENCE SUMMARY

(Erase heading not required.)

Instructions regarding War Diaries and Intelligence Summaries are contained in F.S. Regs., Part II. and the Staff Manual respectively. Title Pages will be prepared in manuscript.

| Place | Date | Hour | Summary of Events and Information | Remarks and references to Appendices |
|---|---|---|---|---|
| ALLOUAGNE | 6/4/16 | | Bath in Billets - Companies had use of baths at ARCHEL - All companies were bathed. | |
| ALLOUAGNE | 7/4/16 | | Bath. took part in a divisional Route March. - The Bath. marched from ALLOUAGNE at 7am. via LOZINGHEM, AUCHEL, CAUCHY-A-LA-TOUR, FERFAY, BELLERY, AUCHY-AU-BOIS, WESTREHEM, FEBVIN PALFART to FLECHIN where they billeted for the night. Billets were found by 'A' Coy consisting of one platoon. The Bath. reached FLECHIN at 1:45p.m. | Advance Party Hazebrouck 5A. |
| FLECHIN | | | | |
| at FLECHIN | 8/4/16 | | Bath. marched to 1st Army Training Area just South of ENGUINEGATTE at 8:15am. - The morning was devoted to Bath. Drill & practice in the attack - during the afternoon the Bath. took part in a practice attack on 140 METRE HILL. 7th Camerons on the left, 10th Gordons on the right - 8th Seaforths in support & 9th Black Watch in reserve. After the attack the Bath. returned to billets at FLECHIN. | " |
| FLECHIN | 9/4/16 | | Bath. marched out at 8:35am. returned to billets at ALLOUAGNE by the same route by which they had marched on 7th. inst. Advance Party (1 Officer (Lieut M. Jackson) & 24 O.R. from each Bath this day)[?]. | |
| ALLOUAGNE | 10/4/16 | | The Bath. witnessed a smoke demonstration on the high ground 1 mile South of BURBURE. 4 October Pym First smoke bomb & demonstration was given by 1 company of Black Watch showing how the attacking force could extricate its concealed by the use of smoke. The Bath this day. | |

# WAR DIARY
## or
## INTELLIGENCE SUMMARY

*(Erase heading not required.)*

Army Form C. 2118.

| Place | Date | Hour | Summary of Events and Information | Remarks and references to Appendices |
|---|---|---|---|---|
| ALLOUAGNE. | 11/4/16 | - | Battn. in billets. Company Training was carried on but owing to the inclemency of the weather training was discontinued whit inspections were carried out. | |
| ALLOUAGNE. | 12/4/16 | . | Battn. in billets. Company Training - "A" Company had the use of the Range. "C" Coy practised the Construction of wire entanglements. | |
| ALLOUAGNE. | 13/4/16 | . | Battn. in billets. Company Training - Capt. E. Robinson R.A.M.C. having met with a serious accident on April 1st whilst on leave to U.K. ceased to be attached to the Battn. | |
| ALLOUAGNE. | 14/4/16 | . | Battn. in billets. Battn. had use of the baths at AUCHEL. | |
| ALLOUAGNE. | 15/4/16 | . | Battn. in billets. Company Training. "B" Coy Musketry on the Range - remaining 3 Coys carried out Company training - Bnd in close extended order &c. | |
| ALLOUAGNE | 16/4/16 | . | Church Parade - inspection of billets by Commanding Officer. | |
| ALLOUAGNE | 17/4/16 | . | Battn. in billets - little training was carried out owing to inclemency of the weather. Brigadier General Marshall took over command of the 44th (Highland) Brigade this day. | |
| ALLOUAGNE | 18/4/16 | . | Battn. in billets. Company training inside Company arrangements. S.O.R. proceeded to Shilly LABOURSE to be attached to 253rd Tunnelling Coy R.E. | |

**WAR DIARY**
or
**INTELLIGENCE SUMMARY**

(Erase heading not required.)

Army Form C. 2118.

Instructions regarding War Diaries and Intelligence Summaries are contained in F.S. Regs., Part II. and the Staff Manual respectively. Title Pages will be prepared in manuscript.

| Place | Date | Hour | Summary of Events and Information | Remarks and references to Appendices |
|---|---|---|---|---|
| ALLOUAGNE | 19/4/16 | | Batt. in billets. Company training - Musketry - Construction of wire entanglements by night. 8 O.R. reports invalided to England & struck off the strength accordingly. Lieut. L. Maclae previously reported missing now reported killed 25/27th Sept 1915. gaz. | |
| ALLOUAGNE | 20/4/16 | | Batt. in billets - Company training. Lieut G. W. Duncan appointed Adjutant vice Capt Butt. Strang posted to Command "B" Coy to date from 29th March 1916. Companies had the use of the Baths at AUCHEL. | |
| ALLOUAGNE | 21/4/16 | | Batt. in billets. The Battn was inspected by G.O.C. 15th Division as follows. "B" Coy (less 1 platoon) Hill marching order. "C" & "D" Coy in Drill Order in Company Drill. Wiring squad of "A" Coy in construction of wire entanglements. Bombing squad of "A" Coy in Attacking & throwing of dummy grenades. Remaining platoon of "B" Coy in musketry firing (a) a Vickers machine (b) a Rifle practice (c) a pistol practice. | |
| ALLOUAGNE | 22/4/16 | | Batt. in billets. Company training. The Battn. was this day inoculated. - 1 Officer (2nd Lieut A. W. Tunstag) & 20 O.R. joined for duty this day. - 1 O.R. was reported invalided to England & struck off the strength. Lieut P. M. O'Sullivan was this day posted to the Medical Charge of the Batt. vice Capt Erskine R.A.M.C. | |

**Army Form C. 2118.**

# WAR DIARY
## or
## INTELLIGENCE SUMMARY

*(Erase heading not required.)*

| Place | Date | Hour | Summary of Events and Information | Remarks and references to Appendices |
|---|---|---|---|---|
| ALLOUAGNE | 23/4/16 | — | Batt in billets. Owing to inoculation men were allowed to remain in their billets all day. | |
| ALLOUAGNE | 24/4/16 | — | Batt in billets. Little training was carried on owing to inoculation. The Commanding Officer, Adjutant & Signalling Officer visited the trenches in the Quarries Section preconnoitring the occupation of the Supporting Battalion (9th Royal Fusiliers) with a view to taking over from that Battalion on the 26th inst. | |
| ALLOUAGNE | 25/4/16 | — | Batt. moved from ALLOUAGNE to BETHUNE as follows — Batt. marched from ALLOUAGNE at 11:10 am in following Ode "C","D","A","B" Coys. Machine Gun Section & Entrained at LILLERS at 12:45pm & arrived at BETHUNE at 1:40pm. The whole Batt. was billeted in the Tobacco Factory BETHUNE. 1st line Transport moved from ALLOUAGNE to BETHUNE via PONT DU REVEILLON & CHOCQUES. | |
| BETHUNE | 26/4/16 | — | Batt. marched from BETHUNE at 9am. to relieve the 9th Royal Fusiliers as Supporting Battalion (Brigade Support) of the Quarry Section. The Cameron Highlanders are on the left & the Ox & Bucks. L.I. on the right sub-section, 10th Gordons still in Reserve in VERMELLES & NOYELLES. The route followed by companies from BETHUNE was SAILLY LABOURSE, ANNEQUIN, VERMELLES, CHAPEL ALLEY. The relief was completed by 2:30pm. The disposition of companies was as follows :— "A" Company O.B. I N of FOSSE WAY. "D" Company O.B. I S of FOSSE WAY. "C" Company O.B. IV & O.B. II. "B" Company CURLEY CRESCENT S of FOSSE WAY. Battalion Head quarters at junction of FOSSE WAY & CURLEY CRESCENT at point G.10.d.4.5. Reference Trench Map 36c N.W. known. |  |
|  |  |  | Battalion Head quarters & Quartermaster's Stores Richebourg at the junction of FOSSE WAY & CURLEY CRESCENT also moved to NOYELLES. | |
|  |  |  | 1st Line Transport & Quartermaster Stores moved to NOYELLES. | |

# WAR DIARY or INTELLIGENCE SUMMARY

Army Form C. 2118.

| Place | Date | Hour | Summary of Events and Information | Remarks and references to Appendices |
|---|---|---|---|---|
| Quarry Section Bn. Support | 26/4/16 | | Relieved 1st Argyll & Sutherland Highrs by Trench Railway from Vermelles to Dump between O.B.4 & Corley Crescent - Water to be drawn from Pump in O.B.4. After relief the day & night passed quietly. There was practically no hostile shelling. | — |
| Quarry Section Bn Support | 27/4/16 | 5.40 a.m. | At this hour a report was received hastily from Brigade Headquarters that "Gas" was reported on right. Indication (g. Black Watch). This was immediately confirmed by reports from O.C. "A" & "D" Coys in O.B.I. All ranks were immediately ordered to "Stand to". Gas clouds passed in a North Westerly direction. The Battalion Gas Sentries cleared by 6.30 a.m. |  |
|  |  | 7.40 a.m. | At this hour "Gas" was again reported by O.C. "A" Coy. All cleared to "Stand to". Returned Gas Alarm. This second gas cloud was slighter than the 1st. The Battalion Area was clear of Gas by 8.15 a.m. The first cloud came in the form of a white mist. The second cloud appeared as a light smoky colour. 30.R. were slightly affected by the gas. An intense bombardment lasted from 5 a.m. to 7 a.m. Gun-wire directed mainly on Vermelles & Le Rutoire Farm. Our trenches in O.B.I., O.B.IV & V.1 & Corley Crescent were untouched. The remainder of the day passed quietly. Communication trenches & working parties found for R.E. &c. details. Work proceeded on Stafford & Communication trenches by 11th & 7th O.B. |  |
| Quarry Section Bn Support | 28/4/16 | | The day passed very quietly. No hostile shelling or activity - Work was done on old Vickys Lines & Communication Trenches. Carrying Parties for ammunition & work to supplies under Brigade Arrangements. Capt. D. W. P. Strang proceeded to Major (temp) to date from 29th March 1916. Gazette for London Gaz. | — |

# WAR DIARY or INTELLIGENCE SUMMARY

Army Form C. 2118.

| Place | Date | Hour | Summary of Events and Information | Remarks and references to Appendices |
|---|---|---|---|---|
| Quarry Section Bde Support | 29/4/16 | — | Bath in Brigade Support. At 4-45 a.m. gas mains reported a suspected gas attack — off gas & smoke helmets were donned. The gas alarm did not however pass over at 5.30 a.m. the Dr stand down pay five. Owing to casualties in 9th Black Watch who are holding the Right subsection 2 platoons of "D" Company were sent up to reinforce 9th Black Watch at 7.30 a.m. Same were also of OR 9th Black Watch. These platoons were relieved at 2.30 p.m. by 2 platoons of "C" Company 8th Seaforth Hdrs. The remainder of the day passed quietly. There was noticeable shelling, working & sniping parties were provided by the Battalion for R.E. & Trench Mortar Batteries. | |
| Dingy Section | 30/4/16 | — | Battn relieved 9th Black Watch in Right Subsection of this sector. The relief commenced at 9.30 a.m. & was complete by 12.45 p.m. This subsection extends from Hero Street (inclusive) to Junction of Turco British with Pilgrims Progress. The disposition of Companies is as follows: from right to left "C" & "D" — "A" & "B" Coys — Companies finding their own supports. 2 platoons of "B" Company are in O.G.I. The Battn now finds its own personnel for the manning of cups left Anvil Battery, 2nd Lieut H.C. Duncan is in command & the personnel consists of Sergeant 4 Corporals & 16 men. The Battery consists of 2 Stokes Guns 2.3.7 guns & 1 4 pounder gun. The Lewis Gun Detachment to man No. 14 Battalion Armaments on 2nd "A" Cordon on the right by the op on the left of a Battalion of the 18th Division on the right. — The 9th Black Watch are in Brigade Support on the left. Lieut Colonel H.J. Cameron H. Gordons in Brigade Reserve. | NI |

2449 Wt. W14957/M90 750,000 1/16 J.B.C. & A. Forms/C.2118/12.

Army Form C. 2118.

# WAR DIARY
### or
# INTELLIGENCE SUMMARY

(Erase heading not required.)

| Place | Date | Hour | Summary of Events and Information | Remarks and references to Appendices |
|---|---|---|---|---|
| QUARRY SECTION. RIGHT SUB-SECTION | 30/4/16. | | The day passed quietly - there being little enemy activity. Work was done on front & support line repairing the parapet & strengthening it where blown in. [signed] | |

CONFIDENTIAL

WAR DIARY

of

8th (Service) Battalion Seaforth Highlanders.

From - 1-5-1916.    to- 31-5-1916.

In the Field.
4-6-1916.

Lieut;Colonel.
Comdg;8th(Service)Bn.Seaforth Highlaners.

# WAR DIARY or INTELLIGENCE SUMMARY

Army Form C. 2118.

| Place | Date | Hour | Summary of Events and Information | Remarks and references to Appendices |
|---|---|---|---|---|
| R/S Sub section Quarry Section. | 1/5/16 | | Hostile Artillery quiet throughout the day – 4.4/5.12 L.M. Battery fired 75 rounds from Stokes Gun on Lookout Crater at G.12.C.5.8. – Enemy retaliates with 3 heavy T.M. bombs but our battery continuing to fire the enemy craters. 11 Rounds were fired from L.H. gun on enemy front line opposite S.E. corner of Hairbourne Loop – one appeared to be accurate, 2 bombs fell in enemy trench – fourth was seen as near but were falling into the trench. A patrol went out at 10.30pm to reconnoitre the far lip of Bacon Crater & found it unoccupied there being no sign of any bombing & listening post. | |
| R/G/G Sub Section Quarry Section. | 2/5/16 | | The disposition of Companies was this day changed. 2 Platoons of "B" Company which were formerly on the left of the line were withdrawn to Putty Trench. This front line is now held by C. D. & A Companies from right to left respectively as per attached sketch (Appendix I). At 12.51pm the enemy blew a mine at G.12.C.U.9 opposite "D" Company. Owing to intermediate ground being exposed to enemy's observation fire it was not considered advisable to attempt to occupy the near lip by day. Arrangements were made in co-operation between Trench Mortars, Vickers & Lewis Guns & a special bombing party under Lieut. J. Milne to cope a working party detailed to dig a sap from Lookout Crescent to the near lip of new crater. Parties of bombers = 2 on each flank followed by bn. the crater occupies the near lip of F.25p.m. They were immediately attacked by enemy bombers & several bombing fights ensued. Enemy trench Mortars were replied to by Dr Trench Mortars for Three Occasions assisting the fires given by our Lieut Richter. At 10.0pm Lieut Milne was wounded & Lieut Darling took command of the bombing party & A.W.40pm Lieut Darling was wounded & Lieut Murray took command of the party. | |

**Army Form C. 2118.**

# WAR DIARY
## or
## INTELLIGENCE SUMMARY
*(Erase heading not required.)*

Instructions regarding War Diaries and Intelligence Summaries are contained in F. S. Regs., Part II. and the Staff Manual respectively. Title Pages will be prepared in manuscript.

| Place | Date | Hour | Summary of Events and Information | Remarks and references to Appendices |
|---|---|---|---|---|
| R.E. Sub Section Quinchy Sector | 2/5/16 | | At 2.30 a.m. the bombers at the Sap head were relieved by the 4th South Lancs Company. Work was continued till daylight by which time the Sap was sufficiently deep to enable the men to be approached by day & bombing posts as now maintained there. The operation was under the general supervision of Captain Forsyth. One man was killed & 3 Officers (mentioned above) & 10 O.R. were wounded. Lieut. D.J. Barton was also wounded whilst in charge of a wiring party on the L.H. Apart from the above operation the enemy were active with French Mortars & Rifle Grenades. Their Snipers were also active. Hostile artillery was quiet. | |
| R.E. Sub Section Quinchy Sector | 3/5/16 | | At 4.45 pm Enemy shelled our front & support Communication trenches with H.E. & Shrapnel. Bombardment lasted for 15 minutes - little damage was done. 4 H.P. L.M. Battery fired 6 rounds from Stokes Gun on new crater at G.12.C.4.9. 3 rounds dropped in crater, 2 appeared to land in or close to enemy Sap head. Rounds were fired from L.H. front-line plate of parapet opposite our Sap head in Look-out Crater - no direct hits obtained. 2 O.R. were wounded by enemy shell fire this day. One was then severely wounded by enemy shell fire - one was then wounded & one made foot round the head of Matheys Sap & between Brecon Crater & Larkin Lane. 50 yards of wire was put up in front of Brookwood Trench. | |
| R.E. Sub-section 4/5/16 Quinchy Sector | | | The Battn. was this day relieved by Gr. Black Watch as per attached Operation Order (Appendix 2). Or relief Battn. moved into Brigade Reserve - "A" "B" Coy. in Vermelles - H'quarters "C" & "D" Coy. Noyelles. Received Wire on mobilisation by a. M.G. 11.45 AM. — 1 O.R. was killed this day by enemy shell fire. M.O. | |

2449  Wt. W14957/M90  750,000  1/16  J.B.C. & A.  Forms/C.2118/12.

Army Form C. 2118.

# WAR DIARY
## or
## INTELLIGENCE SUMMARY
(Erase heading not required.)

Instructions regarding War Diaries and Intelligence Summaries are contained in F. S. Regs., Part II. and the Staff Manual respectively. Title Pages will be prepared in manuscript.

| Place | Date | Hour | Summary of Events and Information | Remarks and references to Appendices |
|---|---|---|---|---|
| Brigade Reserve. Quarry Section | 5/5/16 | - | Batt in Brigade Reserve – Working parties were supplied to 93rd Field Company RE. & fatigue parties for pushing Ration trolleys to ration dump for Battalions in the front & support lines. | Nil. |
| " | 6/5/16 | - | Batt in Brigade Reserve – Lectures were given to Companies on Lewis Gun by Machine Gun Officer with the purpose that every man should know how to fire the Lewis Gun; Working parties were supplied for work on Support line & communication trenches. | Nil. |
| Brigade Reserve | 7/5/16 | - | Batt in Brigade Reserve – | Nil. |
| " | 8/5/16 | - | Companies were this day inspected by Major General the Hon R.H. Murray C.B.C.M.G. Colonel of the Seaforth Highlanders. During the afternoon the Batt. relieved the 9th Black Watch in the Right Subsection Quarry Section (as per attached Operation Order (Appendix 3). The relief was complete by 5 p.m. From 5.30 p.m. to dusk enemy shelled Support, Support, & Reserve trenches with H.E., Shrapnel, & Trench Mortars. Quarry Bay & Princes May were particularly heavily shelled. The disposition of Companies is as before (see Sketch Appendix 1) with the exception that "B" Company were on the left of the line & "A" Company in Battalion Reserve. The W. Yorks H.Q. are on our right & Left. Our right joining up with a Battalion of 16th Division at Stone Street. | Nil. |

# WAR DIARY
## or
## INTELLIGENCE SUMMARY

*(Erase heading not required.)*

Army Form C. 2118.

Instructions regarding War Diaries and Intelligence Summaries are contained in F. S. Regs., Part II. and the Staff Manual respectively. Title Pages will be prepared in manuscript.

| Place | Date | Hour | Summary of Events and Information | Remarks and references to Appendices |
|---|---|---|---|---|
| R/Sub Section Quarry Section | 9/5/16 | | A patrol went out from Devon Lane at 1.30am & patrolled to Newport Sap. Enemy do not occupy continuation of Newport Sap. 11.1/2 L.M. Battery fired 17 rounds from 0° gun in enemy working party behind Newport Sap. 8 rounds from Stokes Gun on Ben Nevis Crater. & 8 rounds from 4.5. gun in retaliation to Enemy Trench Mortar fire. Hostile Artillery more quiet with the exception that New Gun Support Trench was shelled with whizz-bangs apparently from the direction of Hulluch. At 5.10 Pm a party of 250 to 300 Germans left their trenches by platoons at pt. A.7.a.2.4. & marched away behind the village of Cité St Elie. All wore equipment & carried bandolins about 30m per man & rifles. Think was also Dr Cherry Bay & lost on Crescent & on Sap & moving to Crater at G.12.C.4.9 m. Gun Trench was also repaired & parapet & key themes. | Defence Sheet 36 C. N.W. Edition 6 1/20,000 |
| R/Sub Section | 10/5/16 | | At 5 Am. enemy shelled Brockwood Street & Quarry Bay with Shrapnel, H.E. & heavy mortars. The Sap running to Ben Nevis Crater was badly blown in – 10 R. was killed & 6 wounded & crushed as a result of this bombardment. Chapel Alley & the keep front & reserve trench was shelled at 9.30 am but little damage was done. The fired 100 rifle grenades & enemy front line & the range appeared very accurate as many grenades fell in enemy front line. 11/2 L.M. Battery fired 25 rounds from Stokes Gun on S. side of Ben Nevis Crater & struck the enemy trench/in with heavy Mortars & Shrapnel. | " |

**Army Form C. 2118.**

# WAR DIARY
## or
## INTELLIGENCE SUMMARY
*(Erase heading not required.)*

Instructions regarding War Diaries and Intelligence Summaries are contained in F. S. Regs., Part II. and the Staff Manual respectively. Title Pages will be prepared in manuscript.

| Place | Date | Hour | Summary of Events and Information | Remarks and references to Appendices |
|---|---|---|---|---|
| Rt Sub Section Quarry Section | 10/5/16 | 2.15 p.m | An officers patrol went out from Ben Nevis Sap at 2.15 a.m. to reconnoitre enemy and left crater. The patrol was heavily fired on & had to return immediately. The officer & men then crawled out toward the top of the crater to a point where they could see the far side of the crater. The enemy have two bombers posts controlling the crater. A bomb was thrown to try the distance but fell shortly about 10 yards. Neither fire & bombs from his receivers into nearest enemy post but there was no reply. The post being apparently unoccupied. Enemy appear to be working hard in front line also in what appears to be a communication trench at G.12.d.6.8. | Reference Map - Sheet 36c Echelon 1/10000 |
|  |  |  | Enemy artillery was again active about 11 a.m. - Quarry Bay was heavily shelled with H.E, Shrapnel & Shrapnel - 2 O.R. were wounded. The Battn was this day relieved by 5th Battn K.O.S.B. as per attached operation order (Appendix 4). The relief was complete by 2 p.m. a relief companies moved to billets in Bethune. |  |
| Rt Sub Section Quarry Section | 11/5/16 | 5.10 p.m | Orders were received to send a mounted officer to the Brigade headquarters at once. |  |
| Bethune | | 5.50 p.m | All ranks were ordered to "stand to" & orders were received that the Battalion was to be ready to move at shortest notice. |  |
|  |  | 6.50 p.m | Operation Order received from the 4th Inf Bde ordering Battn to move to Vergoignée in preparation to a further move. They state the issues with 100 rounds S.A.A. in addition to that already | at 7.3 p.m |

Army Form C. 2118.

# WAR DIARY
## or
## INTELLIGENCE SUMMARY

*(Erase heading not required.)*

Instructions regarding War Diaries and Intelligence Summaries are contained in F.S. Regs., Part II. and the Staff Manual respectively. Title Pages will be prepared in manuscript.

| Place | Date | Hour | Summary of Events and Information | Remarks and references to Appendices |
|---|---|---|---|---|
| BETHUNE | 11/5/16 | 7.30 p.m. | Carried on till 4.15 p.m. the Battalion marched out of billets to proceed to Vanquinent. At 7.30 p.m. Orders were received to "STAND FAST" at 4 p.m. the Battalion returned to billets. | |
| | | | BETHUNE – All ranks were confined to billets ready to move again at shortest notice. | |
| | | 9 p.m. | At 9 p.m. Orders were received for Battn to move to SAILLY LABOURSE to replace 9th Black Watch who had moved to NOYELLES. The Battalion moved forthwith by 11 p.m. all ranks were in billets at SAILLY LABOURSE. No further operations took place during the night – Was ascertained that at 6 p.m. on 11th inst the Germans had attacked the position of the 103rd Brigade 75th Division, after a very heavy bombardment, but had been almost entirely driven back. | M.H. |
| SAILLY LABOURSE | 12/5/16 | | All ranks were confined to their billets until 2.30 p.m. when the order "Stand down" was received. The Battn was ordered to remain at SAILLY LABOURSE. | M.H. |
| | | | All damage from reprisals of the situation became quite normal. working party of 4 officers & 200 men was supplied for work on Communication trenches at 7 p.m. | M.H. |
| SAILLY LABOURSE | 13/5/16 | | The day was spent in general cleaning up & Kit inspection by Companies. Working parties were supplied for 9th Sptrs No 4. 93rd Field Coy R.E. | M.H. |
| SAILLY LABOURSE | 14/5/16 | | The Battn moved to BETHUNE after attached Operation Order (appendix 5). All ranks were in billets formerly occupied on 11th inst by 11.30 A.M. | |
| BETHUNE | 14/5/16 | 4.30 p.m. | Orders were received to be ready to move at half an hours notice. | |
| | | 6.15 p.m. | Orders were received to send 2 Companies to SAILLY LABOURSE to replace 2 Companies 9th Black Watch. "A" + "B" Coys were ordered to proceed under Capt. J. Murray. | |

# WAR DIARY
## or
## INTELLIGENCE SUMMARY
*(Erase heading not required.)*

Army Form C. 2118.

| Place | Date | Hour | Summary of Events and Information | Remarks and references to Appendices |
|---|---|---|---|---|
| BETHUNE. | 14/5/16 | - | 9 at 8.5pm "A" & "B" Coys saw reports in billets at SAILLY LABOURLE. Nothing further happened during the night. | JW |
| BETHUNE. | 15/5/16 | 4.50pm | At 4.50 pm orders received to withdraw "A" & "B" Coys to BETHUNE & that the Batt. was to be ready to move at one hours notice. "A" & "B" Coys returned to billets BETTONS at 11pm. Nothing further happened during the day. | JW |
| BETHUNE. | 16/5/16 | - | Batt. in Divisional Reserve. Working party of 4 Officers & 200 men supplied at 6.30 pm for 9th Gordons 45th D.B. | JW |
| BETHUNE. | 17/5/16 | - | Batt. in Divisional Reserve. Working party of 2 Officers & 100 men supplied at 8am to 9th Gordons. Bn. to took on Village line. Company training consisting of bombing to aspirts, & gas helmets, Rapid loading & unloading & instruction in Lewis Guns was carried on. | JW |
| BETHUNE. | 18/5/16 | - | Batt. in Divisional Reserve. Company training as above. Working party of 4 officers & 200 men supplied to 45th D.B. & 9th Gordons at 7pm for work on New Support line. Coys were made up as follows. 100 men from "A" Coy & 100 men from "B" Coy under Capt. J.G. Murray. This party remained in VERMELLES during the night. | JW |

# WAR DIARY
## or
## INTELLIGENCE SUMMARY
(Erase heading not required.)

Army Form C. 2118.

| Place | Date | Hour | Summary of Events and Information | Remarks and references to Appendices |
|---|---|---|---|---|
| BERTHONE | 19/5/16 | - | The Batt. this day relieved the 13th Bn The Royal Scots as Supporting Battalion in the HOHENZOLLERN SECTION. As per attached operation order (Appendix 6 & 7) - Relief was complete by 1:30 pm. Carrying parties were found for 170th & 180th Tunnelling Companies. | Appx. |
| BRIGADE SUPPORT HOHENZOLLERN SECTION | 20/5/16 | - | Day passed quietly - Carrying parties were found for Tunnelling Companies. | Nil. |
| BRIGADE SUPPORT HOHENZOLLERN SECTION | 21/5/16 | - | Battalion in Brigade Support. Day passed quietly - Working party of 3 officers 4/100 men were supplied for work on a new trench Munition from Hillock Relay at H.Q. 11.a.3.5h. and towards 40 yards here dug up 3ft to 4ft 6in in depth. While on this working party 2/Lieut L.G. Murray was killed by a machine gun bullet. | Deceased Maj. Sheffield. Appx. |
| BRIGADE SUPPORT HOHENZOLLERN SECTION | 22/5/16 | - | Battalion in Brigade Support. Working party of 3 officers 4/100 men was again supplied as yesterday - New trench was continued for 60 yards & deepened to 4ft 6in in its entire length. | Appx. |
| HOHENZOLLERN SECTION | 23/5/16 | - | The Batt. this day relieved the 1st Batt. Cameron Highlanders in the left subsection HOHENZOLLERN SECTION in accordance with attached operation order (Appendix No 8). Owing to an enemy mine being blown in this He left subsection at 8:15 pm the relief was delayed & was not complete until 3:15 am. In preparation of companies taken as in Appdx. (Appendix No 9) - 8/10th Gordons R.S. are on our right & our Novembers of the day & night passed quietly. Left flank up to post 33rd Division. | Appx. |

2449 Wt. W14957/M90 750,000 1/16 J.B.C. & A. Forms/C.2118/12.

**Army Form C. 2118.**

# WAR DIARY
## or
## INTELLIGENCE SUMMARY
*(Erase heading not required.)*

Instructions regarding War Diaries and Intelligence Summaries are contained in F.S. Regs., Part II. and the Staff Manual respectively. Title Pages will be prepared in manuscript.

| Place | Date | Hour | Summary of Events and Information | Remarks and references to Appendices |
|---|---|---|---|---|
| LEFT SUB-SECTION HOHENZOLLERN SECTION. | 24/5/16 | | Enemy shelled Northampton Trench with H.E. about 8.30a.m. this morning - 20 shells were fired. No damage was done. 21 shells H.E. were also fired (apparently for the direction of CITE ST ELIE) about 9.45a.m. between Bryan St & British Rifle fire. <br><br> 11/11/2 Hostile aeroplane passing over enemy front about 8am today drew a considerable amount of enemy rifle fire & M.G. fire. We availed ourselves of the opportunity & made a retaliation upon the opposed enemy with Light Stokes fire - Rifle firing from S.P. in Crater 5 this morning fires at a German Officer looking through Glasses & claim to have made a hit. <br> 44/2 L.M. Battery fired 98 rounds into 3.4" gun at enemy against G.4.b.3.1 & enemy trenches at G.4.b.4.2 in retaliation to enemy rifle & grenade fire. The remainder of the day passed quietly. There being little activity on either side. JML | |
| LEFT SUBSECTION HOHENZOLLERN Section. | 25/5/16 | | The day was unusually quiet - no hostile shelling. Work was carried on in NORTHAMPTON TRENCH WEST FACE & STICKY TRENCH. Wire was put up to a distance of 50yds from southern flank of RUSSIAN SAP running Northwards. 44/2 L.M. Battery fired 32 rounds from 3.1" gun on enemy crater around G.4.b.3.1. & 12 rounds from enemy 2 inch gun at enemy trenches at G.4.b.4.2 & G.4.b.4.5. in retaliation to rifle grenades &c. JML | |
| LEFT SUBSECTION HOHENZOLLERN SECTION. | 26/5/16 | 1.30am. | An Officer & a sergeant went out at 1.30am. The hostile ground between Craters 3 & 4. The enemy took no selected. Beyond the Wilful of flat ground which can be seen from our trench, the ground dips into a Crater formed by very heavy shells. The patrol was satisfied that it would be almost impossible for the enemy to raid or pass by this direction. Very heavy rain during the day - Northampton Trench & Mud Alley were Affected. No damage was done. JML | |

# WAR DIARY or INTELLIGENCE SUMMARY

Army Form C. 2118.

| Place | Date | Hour | Summary of Events and Information | Remarks and references to Appendices |
|---|---|---|---|---|
| LEFT SUBSECTION HOHENZOLLERN SECTION | 27/5/16 | - | At 6.30am this morn Enemy shelled Mr Trenches at G.4.a.9/2.5/2 with 9.2 Shells from direction of FOSSE 8. Enemy shewed considerable activity with rifle grenades during the afternoon. Their guns destroyed a rank trench opposite party at G.4.b.9.6. Their were action with Rifle Bomb rifle grenades 30 took were fire from the Br. trenches in action with rifle Bomb rifle grenades 30 took were fire from the our attachment at enemy sap opposite trench Back at G.4.6.40. Left Sub Batt fire 16 rounds at enemy trench at G.4.b.42 & G.4.6.45 p.m. by retaliation to enemy. | |
| LEFT SUBSECTION | 28/5/16 | - | Very quiet thing the day. Little activity. At 6.30 pm. message received from 4th Brigade as follows "Aerial reconnaissance states Leave from Douai Rly to Hs gives trains with transport AAA Park of what about 3000 strong ACCS the Spa AAA this is not yet confirmed AAA Br artillery are engaging HAINES AAA message ends. AAA. All units were warned to be exceptionally vigilant but the night passed quietly. | |
| LEFT SUBSECTION HOHENZOLLERN SECTION | 29/5/16 | 3.45 am | By this hour Mr artillery heavy & light carried out an intense bombardment of enemy trenches of 339 division artillery. Enemy replied with 4.2 hr. | |

# WAR DIARY
## or
## INTELLIGENCE SUMMARY.
*(Erase heading not required.)*

Army Form C. 2118.

| Place | Date | Hour | Summary of Events and Information | Remarks and references to Appendices |
|---|---|---|---|---|
| LEFT & 1st SECTION At Nouex les Mines Station | 28/5/16. | | did little damage. Little activity during the morning. At 3 p.m. the enemy shelled Canon Street at its junction with Quay Alley with 4.2.5. - Boyau 111 & 113 were also shelled with H.E. from the direction of ST ELIE. The remainder of the day was quiet. | W. |
| LEFT & 1st SECTION HHH 24 Loos Section | 29/5/16. | | Enemy active with aerial darts, especially along Northampton Trench. Our bombers & snipers were active against enemy sniper plates opposite HOG'S BACK. 4 p.m. Our battery fires 13 rounds at enemy craters at G.4.b.4.8. in retaliation for enemy aerial darts. 2 rounds at suspected enemy emplacement at G.4.b.5.5. At 11 p.m. a patrol went out for ft-6.4.b.2.8 & listened close to enemy's parapet from 2.30 of which there were heard in every front line Aberdeen & iron also heard. It is thought that this bombing was used to drown up trolleys which were heard being in iron rails. W. |

# WAR DIARY
## or
## INTELLIGENCE SUMMARY.
(Erase heading not required.)

Army Form C. 2118.

| Place | Date | Hour | Summary of Events and Information | Remarks and references to Appendices |
|---|---|---|---|---|
| LEFT SUBSECTION HERZEELE Sector | 2/5/16 | | Between 8.45 a.m. & 9.30 a.m. about 8 & 25 trench mortars & rifle grenades fired behind Northampton trench from the direction of C.75 & T E1.5. They were dealt with at once along the length of Northampton trench. No damage was done. The bombers were of use with rifle grenades & Bott's fired from C of attachment. A special duel with L.T.H's were made. Enemy acting with aerial darts we replied with light trench mortars. The remainder of the day was very quiet. | |

Appendix I

RIGHT BAT'N FRONT

MERTHYR SAP
2 Platoons "C" Coy
GUN TRENCH
BRECON TR
LANE TR
SUPPORT
2 Platoons "C" Coy
HAIR PIN SAP
FARM LANE
2 Platoons "D" Coy
OLD CRESCENT
PIGGERIES
DUDLEY TRENCH
STONE ST
DEVON LANE TRENCH
CHAPEL ALLEY
2 Platoons "B" Coy
PUTTY TRENCH
BROCK WOOD TRENCH
1 Platoon "A" Coy
WISE WAY
DUG OUT ROAD
3 Platoon "A" Coy
QUARRY SAP
CHAPEL ALLEY
DEVON LANE
2 Platoons "B" Coy O.C.
Bath Headquarters

Secret  Operation Order  Appendix 2 Copy No 8
by
Lieut: Colonel. N.A. Thomson.
Comdg: 8th (Service) Bn. Seaforth Highlanders.

1. The 8th Bn Seaforth Highlanders will be relieved by the 9th The Black Watch to-morrow 4th May, 1916.

2. "A" Coy will be relieved by "A" Coy 9th The Black Watch.
   "B" Coy    "    "    "    "  "B" Coy  "   "    "    "
   "C" Coy    "    "    "    "  "C" Coy  "   "    "    "
   "D" Coy    "    "    "    "  "D" Coy  "   "    "    "

3. Companies, Lewis Guns & Trench Mortar Detachment will send Guides, 1 per platoon, 1 per Gun to junction of CHAPEL ALLEY & O.G.1 at the following times:—

   Signallers .. 8 a.m.         A. Coy. 10 a.m.
   Lewis Guns. 8.30 a.m.        B. Coy. 10.30 a.m.
   C. Coy.     9. a.m.          Headquarters. 11 a.m.
   D. Coy.     9.30 a.m.        Trench Mortar Battery 11.30 a.m.

4. On relief, Coy's will move as follows:—
   Headquarters, Lewis Gun Detachment, "C" & "D" Coy's to NOELLES via DEVON LANE, O.B.1, STANSFIELD RD, VERMELLES, PHILOSOPHE, NOELLES.
   "A" & "B" to VERMELLES via BRESLAU AVENUE, STAFFORD LANE, O.B.1. STANSFIELD ROAD, VERMELLES.
   West of VERMELLES, all movement will be by platoons at 200 yards interval.
   On relief the personnel of TRENCH MORTAR BATTERY will rejoin their Coy's in billets.

5. Trench Stores will be handed over & receipt taken and forwarded to Battalion H.Q. by 9 a.m. 5th May, 1916.

George W. Duncan
Lieutenant.
Adjutant 8th Bn Seaforth High'rs

Copy No 1 - "A" Coy.
  "   "  2 - "B" Coy
  "   "  3 - "C" Coy
  "   "  4 - "D" Coy.
  "   "  5 - M.G.O.
  "   "  6 - T.M.O.
  "   "  7 - O.C. 9th B.W.
  "   "  8 - File.

SECRET                                                    Copy.No.8.

*Appendix 3*

OPERATION ORDER
by
Lt.Colonel.N.A.Thomson,Comdg;8th Bn.Seaforth Highlanders,7th May,16.
------------------------------------------------------------------

1. The 8th Bn.Seaforth Highlanders will releive the 9th Bn.
   Black Watch in the Right Sub-Section,QUARRIES SECTION to-morrow
   8th May,1916.

2. Disposition of Companies will be as follows:-
   "C" Company on the right.
   "D" Company in the centre.
   "B" Company on the left.
   "A" Company in reserve.

3. Companies,Lewis Gun Detachment and Trench Mortar Battery will
   pass Church VERMELLES at the following hours:-
   "C" Company - 2-30.P.M.
   "D" Company - 2-45.P.M.
   "B" Company - 3.P.M.
   "A" Company - 3-15.P.M.
   Lewis Gun Detachment - 3-30.P.M.
   Trench Mortar Battery -3-45.P.M.
   Route-VERMELLES,CHAPEL ALLEY.

4. Advanced parties of 1 Officer and 1.N.C.O per Company and the
   Bombing Officer will proceed to the trenches to-morrow at 9.A.M.
   to take over Trench stores and Bomb stores respectively.

5. Blankets in bundles of ten and packs of "C" & "D" Companies will
   be stacked at Quartermasters Stores NOYELLES by 7.A.M.to-morrow,
   8th inst.
   Blankets and packs of "A" & "B" Companies will be stacked at
   Company Quartermaster Stores VERMELLES by 7.A.M.to-morrow,8th inst.
   The Transport Officer will arrange to collect these stores.

6. All trench stores will be taken over and receipts forwarded to
   Battalion Headquarters by 9.A.M.,8th May,QOQY.


In the Field.                          *George W Duncan*
7-5-1916.                                          Lt`& Adjutant.
                              8th Bn.Seaforth Highlanders.

SECRET.    Copy No. 9

## OPERATION ORDER
by
Major.G.M.Lumsden,Comdg;8th Bn.Seaforth Highlanders. 9-5-1916.

1. The 8th Bn.Seaforth Highlanders will be relieved by the 8th Bn.K.O.S.Borders on the 11th May,1916.

2. Companies will be releived in the following order:-
   "C" Coy by "C" Coy,8th Bn.K.O.S.B's.
   "A" Coy by "B" Coy,8th Bn.K.O.S.B's.
   "D" Coy by "D" Coy,8th Bn.K.O.S.B's.
   "B" Coy by "A" Coy,8th Bn.K.O.S.B's.
   Guides(1 per platoon)will be at junction of CHAPEL ALLEY and FOSSE WAY at 12 noon on the 11th inst to guide companies of 8th Bn.K.O.S.B's.

3. On relief,companies will move to BETHUNE as follows:-
   "C" & "D" Coy's- D VON LANE,O.B.5.,STANSFIELD ROAD,CROSS ROADS Pt.L.6.c.,SAILLY LABOURSE,BETHUNE.
   "A" & "B" Coy's-BRESLAU AVENUE,STAFFORD LANE,O.B.5.,STANSFIELD ROAD,CROSS ROADS Pt L.6.c.,SAILLY LABOURSE,BETHUNE.
   All movements East of SAILLY LABOURSE will be by platoons at 200 yards interval.

4. Advanced parties of 8th K.O.S.B's will arrive at Junction CHAPEL ALLEY & FOSSE WAY at 4.P.M.,10th May,1916. 1 guide per company will be sent to meet them.

5. Billeting parties,4 per company & 1 for Headquerters will parade at Battalion Headquarters at 12-30.P.M.,on 10th May and proceed under Lieut;D.B.Macauley to reach Headquarters 8th K.O.S.B's at 5.P.M.,10th May.

6. All surplus Mess Kits will be sent down with ration trolleys on the night of the 10th inst.
   Three limbers will be detailed by the Transport Officer to be at Brewery VERMELLES at 2 P.M.,on the 11th inst to take any remaining kit or dixchies to BETHUNE.

7. All trench stores will be handed over & receipts taken. Receipts will be forwarded to Battalion Headquarters by 9.A.M.,12th May.

                                            Lt & Adjutant.
                                    8th Bn.Seaforth Highlanders.

Copy.No.1....C.O.
    "    " 2....A Coy.
    "    " 3....B Coy.
    "    " 4....C Coy.
    "    " 5....D Coy.
    "    " 6....Transport Officer.
    "    " 7....Quartermaster.
    "    " 8....O.C.8th B.K.O.S.B's.
    "    " 9....File.

SECRET.   Operation Order.                Copy No. 8
                by
              Major G.H. Lumsden.        Appendix 5
            Cmdg 8th Seaforth H'rs.      13th May 1916.

1. The 8th Seaforth H'rs. will move to BETHUNE tomorrow 14th
   inst as follows :-  "A" Coy  9 a.m.
                       "B" Coy  9.15 a.m.
                       "C" Coy  9.30 a.m.
                       "D" Coy & M.G. Section  9.45 a.m.

2. Billeting Parties (1 per Company) will parade at Battn.
   Headquarters at 8 a.m. 14th inst.

3. Blankets will be rolled in bundles of ten labelled &
   taken to Quartermasters Stores by 6 a.m.
   Officers Valises to be in Quartermasters Stores by 8.30 a.m.
   Mess Boxes will be collected at 8.30 a.m.

4. Men will carry their packs.
   SHRAPNEL HELMETS & KILT APRONS WILL BE WORN.


Copy No 1. O.C. "A" Coy.              George W Dunnes
  "    "  2. O.C. "B" Coy.                 Lieut & Adj
  "    "  3. O.C. "C" Coy.             8th Seaforth H'rs.
  "    "  4. O.C. "D" Coy.
  "    "  5. Transport Officer
  "    "  6. Machine Gun Officer
  "    "  7. Quartermaster.
  "    "  8. File.

SECRET.

COPY NO. 9.

Appendix 6

## Operation Order No. 1

by

Major G. M. Lumsden.

Commdg. 8th (S) Bn. Seaforth Highlanders

18 May 1916

1. The 8th (S) Bn. Seaforth Highlanders will relieve the 13th Bn. The Royal Scots, as Supporting Battalion in the HOHENZOLLERN SECTION, on 19th May 1916.

2. The disposition of Companies will be as follows:-
   - "A" Coy. — VILLAGE LINE with one platoon in JUNCTION KEEP.
   - "B" Coy. — RAILWAY RESERVE Trench with one platoon in CENTRAL KEEP.
   - "C" and "D" Coys. — LANCASHIRE TRENCH ("C" Coy. on the Right. "D" Coy. on the Left.)

   Battn. Hdqrs. are situated in BARTS ALLEY - Pt. G.9.a.7.8.

3. Companies will march from BETHUNE to-morrow as follows:-
   - Starting Point......... Tobacco Factory.
   - Time.................... 8.15 a.m.
   - Order of March........ Details of "A" and "B" Coys, "C", "D" Coys. Lewis Gun Detachment, Headquarters.
   - Route................... SAILLY LA BOURSE, CROSS ROADS, L.6.C. ANNEQUIN, VERMELLES, CLARKES KEEP.

   Companies will move off at 15 mins. interval.
   All movements E. of SAILLY LA BOURSE will be by platoons at 200 yards interval.
   Guides (1 per platoon) will be at CLARKES KEEP at 10.45 a.m.

4. O.C. "C" Coy. will detail a N.C.O. to take over Brigade Ammunition and Bomb Stores at CLARKES KEEP at 11 a.m.

5. Capt. G. Murray will arrange for the party of 200 men billetted in VERMELLES on the night of 18th May, to arrive at CLARKES KEEP by platoons at 200 yds. interval in the order "A" - "B" Coys. The leading platoon of "A" Coy. to arrive at 10.45 a.m.

6. Blankets will be rolled in Bundles of 10, labelled and taken to Divisional Quartermasters Stores together with packs by 6.30 a.m. Officers Valises, together with any surplus mess-kit, will be taken to Div. Quartermasters stores by 7.30 a.m.

7. The Transport Officer will place one limber at the disposal of each Coy. for transporting mess boxes, dutchies etc. These limbers will report at Coy. Hd. Qrs. at 7.30 a.m. and will proceed to BREWERY, VERMELLES.
   All mess servants and cooks must march with their Coys. as far as the BREWERY, VERMELLES where they will fall out and await the arrival of Transport.

8. 1st Line Transport will move to SAILLY LA BOURSE at 10 a.m. and take over from 13th Bn. The Royal Scots there.

9. Receipts for Trench Stores will be rendered to Bn. Hd. Qrs. by 9 a.m. 20 mai

COPY No. 1  O.C. "A" Coy.
        2  O.C. "B" Coy.
        3  O.C. "C" Coy.
        4  O.C. "D" Coy.
        5  Machine Gun Officer
        6  Trench Mortar Officer
        7  Transport Officer
        8  Quartermaster
        9  War Diary
       10  File.

George W Duncan
Lieut.,
Adjutant. 8th Bn. Seaforth Highrs.

Appendix 7.

SECRET.
8th Seaforth A.O. D 535.

O.C. All Companies.

1. Reference Operation Order No 1 issued today – the disposition of Companies will be as follows & not as therein stated –:

   "A" Company – "Lancashire Trench" with 1 platoon in Junction Keep.

   "B" Company – Railway Reserve Trench with 1 platoon in Central Keep.

   "C" & "D" Companies – "Lancashire Trench."

George W Duncan.
Lieut & Adj.
8th Seaforth Hrs.

18/5/16.

Secret

Copy No. 7

# OPERATION ORDER No 2. Appendix 8
### by Lieut. Col. N. A. Thomson
### Commdg. 8th (S) Battn Seaforth Highlanders.
### — 22nd May, 1916 —

1. The 8th Seaforth Highrs. will relieve the 7th Cameron Highlanders to-morrow, May. 23rd 1916.

2. Companies will relieve as follows:—
   "A" Coy. 8th Seaforth Highrs. will relieve "A" Coy. 7th Cameron Hrs. on Left of Firingline
   "B" Coy. 8th Seaforth Hrs. will relieve "D" Coy. 7th Cameron Hrs. in Centre of Firingline
   "C" Coy. 8th Seaforth Hrs. will relieve "C" Coy. 7th Cameron Hrs. on Right of Firingline
   "D" Coy. 8th Seaforth Hrs. will relieve "B" Coy. 7th Cameron Hrs. in Reserve.

   Companies will relieve in the following order:—
   "C" "B" "A" and "D" Companies.
   2 Lewis Guns will follow "C" Coy; and 2 Lewis Guns will follow "A" Coy
   Guides (4 per Coy.) will be at Junction of QUARRY ALLEY and CANNON STREET at 9 a.m. for "C" "A" and "D" Coys. and Lewis Guns — for "B" Coy. at Junction of QUARRY ALLEY and RAILWAY RESERVE TRENCH at 9.20 a.m.
   Route for "C" and "B" Coys:— QUARRY ALLEY and GUILDFORD TRENCH.
   Route for "A" Coy — QUARRY ALLEY and MUD ALLEY.
   Route for "D" Coy — QUARRY ALLEY.

3. Platoons of "A" and "B" Coys. at present garrisoning CENTRAL and JUNCTION KEEPS will not move until relieved by platoons of the 7th Cameron Highrs.

4. Parties to take over Trench Stores will proceed to Companies of 7th Cameron Highrs. at 7 a.m. to-morrow.
   Receipts for Trench Stores to be rendered to Battn. Headquarters by 6 p.m. 23rd inst.

George W Duncan
Lieut.
Adjutant 8th Battn Seaforth Highlanders

Copy No. 1 O.C. "A" Coy.
" 2. O.C. "B" Coy.
" 3. O.C. "C" Coy.
" 4. O.C. "D" Coy.
" 5. M.G. Officer.
" 6. O.C. 7th Cameron Highrs.
" 7. War Diary.
" 8. File.

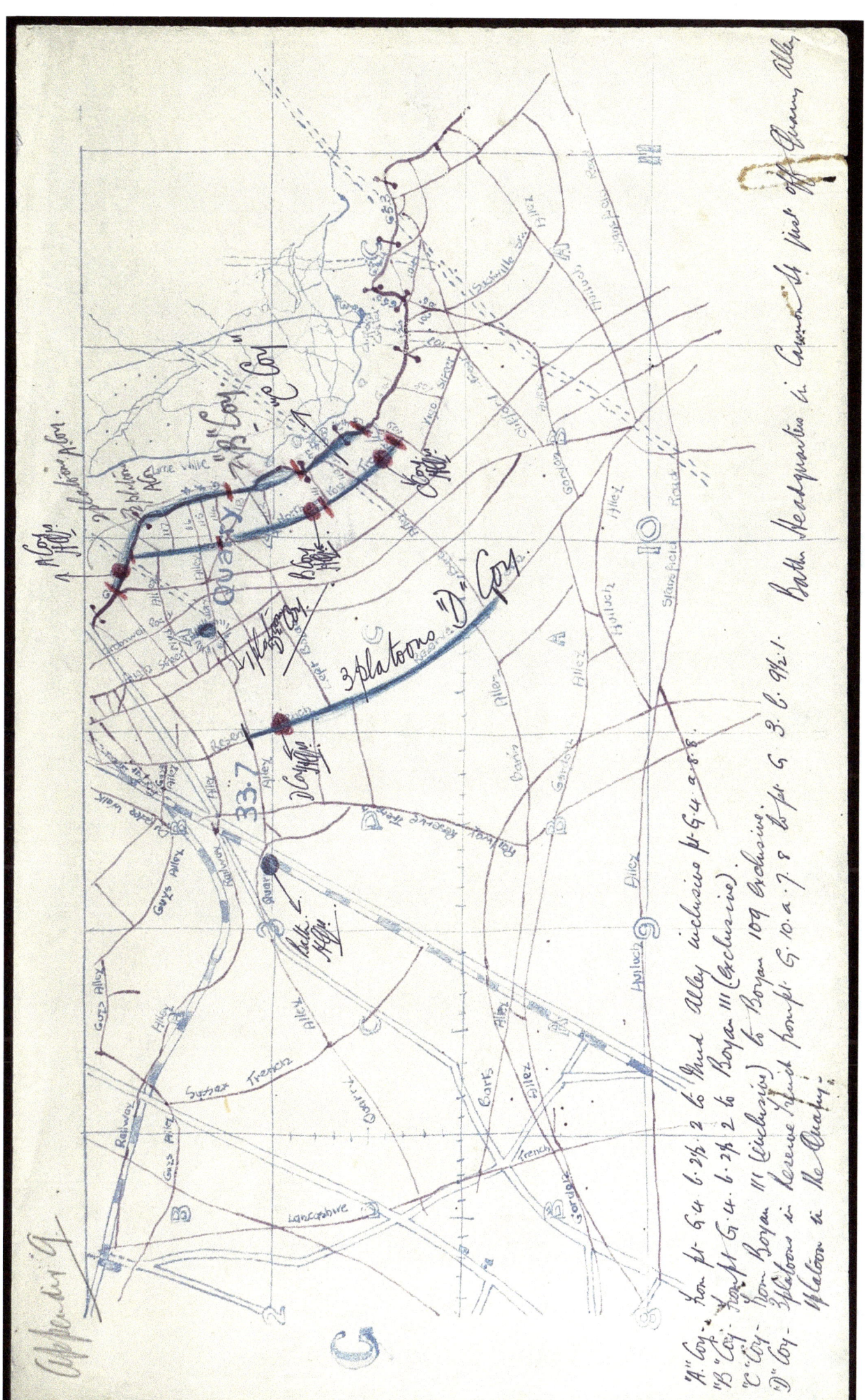

out leaflets
Vol 3
15F/D/3

44

7.7
15M

CONFIDENTIAL.

WAR DIARY

of

8th (S) BATTN SEAFORTH HIGHLANDERS

from 1st June 1916 to 30th June 1916.

VOLUME. XII.

In the field.

Ian Henderson Lieut-Colonel.
Cmdg 8th Seaforth Highlanders.

# WAR DIARY or INTELLIGENCE SUMMARY

Army Form C. 2118.

| Place | Date | Hour | Summary of Events and Information | Remarks and references to Appendices |
|---|---|---|---|---|
| LEFT SUBSECTION HOHENZOLLERN SECTION | 1/6/16 | | A quiet day - except for slight enemy artillery activity between 6.45am & 7.30am when Mad Alley trench was shelled with 20 4.2's from the direction of Cité St Elie. | |
| | | | Our trench mor action with rifle Grenade bombs fired from Coy attachment of enemy saphead - several direct hits were obtained. | |
| | | | Lieut Ch Battery fired 32 rounds at enemy trenches at G.6.b.4.2. in retaliation for enemy T.M. | |
| | | | Quiet Night. | |
| LEFT SUBSECTION HOHENZOLLERN SECTION | 2/6/16 | 6.45 PM | Enemy being active with trench mortars. This & Support Trench between G.4.d.5.3, 7.6.9, & 5.6. Enemy active with aerial darts during afternoon. Our bombers replies with bombs & rifle Grenades. Lieut Ch Battery fires 45 rounds at enemy trenches at G.U.b.4.2 & G.U.b.4.5. - Remainder of day & night quiet. | |
| LEFT S. SUBSECTION HOHENZOLLERN SECTION | 3/6/16 | - | At 2 PM enemy shelled our trenches between Boyan 112 & Mud Alley with about 30 L.T.M. shells from direction of Fosse 8. | |
| | | 10.15 PM | Our trenches at G.U.A.8½ & 11a "four pounded" for about pt. G.U.b.9.5. (Shells 1ft 4 in. height). | |
| | | | Enemy were unusually active with rifle Grenades during the afternoon - We replied with rifle Grenades & L.T.M.'s 47 rounds being fired by Lieut Ch. Batter on enemy trenches. | |

Army Form C. 2118.

# WAR DIARY
or
# INTELLIGENCE SUMMARY.
(Erase heading not required.)

Instructions regarding War Diaries and Intelligence Summaries are contained in F. S. Regs., Part II. and the Staff Manual respectively. Title pages will be prepared in manuscript.

| Place | Date | Hour | Summary of Events and Information | Remarks and references to Appendices |
|---|---|---|---|---|
| LEFT SUB-SECTION Mt HENDALLEN SECTOR | 4/6/16 | – | The Battn was this day relieved by the 10th H.L.I. in accordance with Operation Order No 3 attached (Appendix) the relief was complete at 10.40 a.m. – The Battn time reported in billets at LABOURSE by 1.30pm. – 2nd/Lieut L. M. Cameron & the Battn Snipers proceeded to Company for a course of instruction in Sniping. | |
| LABOURSE | 5/6/16 | – | Battn in billets – The day was devoted to general cleaning up. – | |
| LABOURSE | 6/6/16 | – | Battn in billets – training resumed – Working parties found for 4th Field Coy RE | |
| LABOURSE | 7/6/16 | – | Training under Company arrangements. Machine Gunners and a Machine Gun officer & Instructor under Bombing Officer. | |
| LABOURSE | 8/6/16 | – | Battn in billets – training as above. | |
| LABOURSE | 9/6/16 | – | Battn in billets – Working parties supplied as detailed by 44th Infantry Brigade. | |
| LABOURSE | 10/6/16 | – | Battn in billets – | |
| LABOURSE | 11/6/16 | – | Battn in billets – Church parade at 10.30 am. | |

# WAR DIARY or INTELLIGENCE SUMMARY

Army Form C. 2118.

| Place | Date | Hour | Summary of Events and Information | Remarks and references to Appendices |
|---|---|---|---|---|
| LABOURSE | | | | |
| R.I.S.B.Section Hulluch Section | 12/6/16 | | HULLUCH<br>The Battn. this day relieved the 13th Royal Scots in the R.I. Subsection Hulluch Section<br>In accordance with Operation Order No.1 attached (Appendix 2). One Company of K.R.R. Lancs. Regt. was attached to the Batn. for instruction - 1 Platoon being with each company.<br>SEAFORTH HIGHLANDERS:- The disposition of Companies was as follows:- R.I. Firing line "D" Coy. Centre Firing line "C" Coy. Left Firing line "B" Coy. Support Coy. "A" Coy. - Bomb. Sections of Batt. Section are as follows - Ten. Din. ALLEY (northern) 16 Bomb. 75 (northern) fire.<br>The day passed very quietly. Little activity on either side. | |
| R.I.Sub.Section Hulluch Section | 13/6/16 | | Another very quiet day. Hostile artillery working 244/1 R.R. Batty fired 20 rounds at enemy trench at H.13.c.5/8.3. 1.H.13.c.5/8.5. Batteries reined direct hits. M.W. | |
| R.I. Subsection Hulluch Section | 14/6/16 | | A quiet day - at 2.30 A.M. the enemy flew a small mine at H.13.a.2 1/2. - no craters is visible. Little damage was done.<br>Our bombers were active with rifle Grenades - 44/1 L.R. Batty fired 10 rounds for Stokes Gun in retaliation to enemy aerial darts - One direct hit was obtained on enemy front line. Much work is being done by us in retraining support line communication. M.W. | |
| R.I. Subsection Hulluch Section | 15/6/16 | | Another quiet day - At 11.5 pm the enemy opening a trench L Mortar Bays 3 & 4 (H.13.c.3.8.73). No damage was caused to our trenches or Bays. The explosion took place in front of | |

# WAR DIARY or INTELLIGENCE SUMMARY

Army Form C. 2118.

(Erase heading not required.)

| Place | Date | Hour | Summary of Events and Information | Remarks and references to Appendices |
|---|---|---|---|---|
| R1 SUB SECTION HULLUCH SECTION | 15/9/16 | | 14 present craters to be formed to new crater. Our Trench mortars were active both with rifle Grenades - good practice being made - on Lewis Guns fired on enemy working party at A.13.c.5.5½. Light M.G. Battery fired 19 rounds at enemy frontline G.13.c.6.8 & G.13.c.6.6. ¼. All were observed. | |
| R SUBSECTION HULLUCH Section | 16/9/16 | | "B" Coy 11th Northants left the trenches in accordance with Operation Order No 2 (Appendix 2) & "A" Coy 13th East Surrey Regt. fired front the Battalion to instruction - The Battalion this day relieved by 4th Cameron Highlanders in accordance with Operation Order No 3 (Appendix 4) - The relief was completed by 4 pm. The Battalion moved back into Brigade Support. The day was quiet there being little activity on either side. Trench Carrying parties were provided for Gunville Companies during the night. Civil Battn in Bde. support - Rechefells. The whole Battalion were employed on working or carrying parties for themselves & 14th field Company R.E. | |
| BRIGADE SUPPORT HULLUCH SECTION | 17/9/16 | | On the night of 17th/18th inst. a special carrying party of 6 officers, 36 NCO's & 384 men were detailed for carrying & installing "LOOS NAILERS" (GAS CYLINDERS) into front trenches. This party | |

Army Form C. 2118.

# WAR DIARY
or
## INTELLIGENCE SUMMARY.
(Erase heading not required.)

Instructions regarding War Diaries and Intelligence Summaries are contained in F.S. Regs., Part II. and the Staff Manual respectively. Title pages will be prepared in manuscript.

| Place | Date | Hour | Summary of Events and Information | Remarks and references to Appendices |
|---|---|---|---|---|
| BRIGADE SUPPORT HULLUCH SECTION | 17/6/16. | | Was divided into 6 groups consisting of 1 Officer & NCO & 50 men each & works made special distribution issued by 1st Infantry Brigade. This party commenced work at 10.15 pm & finished at 4 am. | Ap. |
| BRIGADE SUPPORT HULLUCH SECTION | 18/6/16. | | Batt in Bde Support - Working parties supplied as on 17th inst - The special carrying parts of 6 Officers, 35 NCOs & 350 men were engaged on the same work as on 17th inst. | Ap. |
| BRIGADE SUPPORT HULLUCH SECTION | 19/6/16. | | Batt in Bde Support - Working parties supplied as above - The special carrying parts were reduced to 5 Officers, 30 NCO's & 320 men - work was carried out as on the two previous nights. Nothing further to report. | Ap. |
| LEFT SUBSECTION HULLUCH SECTION | 20/6/16. | | The Battn this day relieved the 8/10th Gordon Hdrs in the left Subsection Hulluch section in accordance with attached operation order No. 4 (Appendix 5) - Relief was complete by 12 noon. The disposition of Companies to in so far attached sketch (Appendix 6). "A" Coy 13th East Surrey Regt left the trenches & "B" Coy 11th K.R.R. came became attached to the Battn for training in the front line as a Company (2 platoons in OBI & 2 platoons in OGI) as per attached operation order No 5 (Appendix 7). The day was quiet - little activity on either side | Ap. |

T2134. Wt. W708—776. 500000. 4/15. Sir J. C. & S.

# WAR DIARY
## or
## INTELLIGENCE SUMMARY.
*(Erase heading not required.)*

Army Form C. 2118.

Instructions regarding War Diaries and Intelligence Summaries are contained in F. S. Regs., Part II. and the Staff Manual respectively. Title pages will be prepared in manuscript.

| Place | Date | Hour | Summary of Events and Information | Remarks and references to Appendices |
|---|---|---|---|---|
| LEFT SUB SECTION Midwich Section | 21/6/16 | | "B" Coy 11th R.S. Lanc: Regt. relieves "C" Coy 5th Seaforth Highlanders in the Pt. Firing line in accordance with Operation Order No. 6 (Appendix 8). The day was quiet except for enemy trench mortars during the afternoon — enemy bay being heavily shelled. Wiring was continued along our front. Much work is in progress repairing front & support line trenches which are in a very bad state. | |
| LEFT SUB SECTION Midwich Section | 22/6/16 | | A quiet day — nothing to report. | |
| LEFT SUB SECTION Midwich Section | 23/6/16 | | "B" Coy 11th K.O.R. Lanc: Regt. was relieved by "B" Coy 13th East Lancs. Regt. in accordance with Operation Order No. 4 (Appendix 9). There was activity with Heavy Trench Mortars — otherwise a quiet day. | |
| LEFT SUB SECTION Midwich Section | 24/6/16 | | Our artillery were active during the day & night — bombardments were carried out on enemy machine gun emplacements & on enemy communications. Trench Mortars bombarded enemy wire at G.12.c.4.0 & on enemy front line at various points opposite our front. Observation was difficult during to enemy retaliation & fairly light & heavy retaliation by enemy | |

Army Form C. 2118.

# WAR DIARY
or
## INTELLIGENCE SUMMARY.
*(Erase heading not required.)*

Instructions regarding War Diaries and Intelligence Summaries are contained in F.S. Regs., Part II. and the Staff Manual respectively. Title pages will be prepared in manuscript.

| Place | Date | Hour | Summary of Events and Information | Remarks and references to Appendices |
|---|---|---|---|---|
| LEFT SubSECT. Hulluch Section | 24/6/16 | | With trenches & artillery. Our Lewis Guns were active on enemy wire front line. | |
| LEFT SubSection. Hulluch Section. | 25/6/16 | | Our artillery affair active – Orders were issued for operations in accordance with Operation No 8 attached. These orders were cancelled owing to unfavorable condition of the wind. Our light Mortars & Machine Guns were active on enemy wire & front line in fact. | |
| LEFT SubSection 26/6/16 Hulluch Section. | 26/6/16 | | Our artillery & trench Mortars affair active Artillery wire cutting & on enemy Guns harasses enemy front line during the night. "B" Coy 13th East Surrey Regt. were relieved by D Coy 8th Seaforth H'rs in accordance with Operation Order No 8 (appendix A) During the night 26th/27th June Operations were carried out in accordance with 44th Brigade Operation Order No 63 (appendix B) – The operation was carried out by the 9th Black Watch & on our right & did not affect our battalion. | |
| LEFT SubSection Hulluch Section | 27/6/16 | | Our artillery trench Mortars & Lewis Guns were again very active – Operations as ordered for 25th/26th inst. took place – but were carried out on the night of 27th/28th as there were no Loos invaders on our front & little artillery preparation only, a small | |

# WAR DIARY
## or
## INTELLIGENCE SUMMARY.

Army Form C. 2118.

(Erase heading not required.)

| Place | Date | Hour | Summary of Events and Information | Remarks and references to Appendices |
|---|---|---|---|---|
| LEFT SUBSECTOR HULLUCH SECTOR | 27/6/16 | | Patrol went out from "A" Coy from Ben Nevis SAP & working along its West side to the small mud craters which from it they endeavoured to cut out & capture a party of the enemy which had been seen out in this vicinity. The enemy party was not however discovered, possibly having been put off by the general bombardment of the enemy lines. In consequence the wire & the patrol returned safely to our trenches. | |
| LEFT SUBSECTOR HULLUCH SECTOR | 28/6/16 | | The Battalion was this day relieved by 1st/5th K.R.Rifles in accordance with Operation Order No. 9 (Appendix No. 13). On relief the Batt. moved to SAILLY LABOURSE with "C" Coy in Noyelles. | |
| SAILLY LABOURSE | 29/6/16 | | Batt. in billets — Day devoted to general cleaning up. | |
| SAILLY LABOURSE | 30/6/16 | | Batt. in billets — Training, musketry, Coy arrangements — Stretch Drill, Handling of Arms & practice in the use of gas helmets. | |

SECRET.                                          Copy No. 9

## OPERATION ORDER No.3
by
Lt.Colonel N.A.Thomson, Comdg; 8th Bn.Seaforth Highlanders, 3rd June, 16.

APPENDIX I

1. The 8th Bn.Seaforth Highlanders will be relieved by the 10/11th Highland Light Infantry to-morrow, 4th June, 1916.

2. Companies will be relieved in the following order:-

   "D" Coy, 8th Bn.Seaforth Highdrs by "D" Coy 10/11th H.L.I.
   "C"    "    "    "         "       "  "C"  "    "     "
   "A"    "    "    "         "       "  "A"  "    "     "
   "B"    "    "    "         "       "  "B"  "    "     "

   Guides (4 per Company) will be sent to CLARKS KEEP at 8.A.M. 4th June to guide incoming Companies.
   Route for relieving Companies of 10/11th H.L.I.:-
   "D" & "C" Coy's - QUARRY ALLEY and GUILFORD TRENCH.
   "A" Coy -        QUARRY ALLEY and MUD ALLEY.
   "B" Coy -        QUARRY ALLEY.

3. On reliefs, Companies will move to LABOURSE via HARTS ALLEY, VERSAILLES, CROSS ROADS L.G.s., SAILLY LABOURSE.
   All movements East of SAILLY LABOURSE will be by platoons at 200 yards interval.

4. All surplus Mess kits will be sent down Glyn Ration Trolleys on the night of the 3rd inst.
   3 Limbers will be detailed by the Transport Officer to be at CLARKS KEEP at 8.A.M.4th inst to take any remaining kits or dischies to LABOURSE.
   All cooks and Mess servants will march under the Master-Cook after having loaded up Transport at CLARKS KEEP.

5. All trenches, latrines etc; must be left scrupulously clean and certificates obtained from incoming Company Commanders that they are so.

6. All trench stores will be handed over and receipts taken. Receipts will be forwarded to Battalion Headquarters by 5.P.M. 5th June.

7. Completion of reliefs will be reported by wire to Battalion Headquarters.

                                              Lieutenant,
                        Adjutant, 8th Bn.Seaforth Highlanders.

Copy No. 1.....C.O.
    "     2.....O.C.10/11th Highland Light Infantry.
    "     3.....A.Coy.
    "     4.....B.Coy.
    "     5.....C.Coy.
    "     6.....D.Coy.
    "     7.....Transport Officer.
    "     8.....Quartermaster.
    "     9.....War Diary.

SECRET — OPERATION ORDER No 1 —    COPY No 8

APPENDIX II

Lieut. Col. by N. A Thomson
Commdg 8th (S) Bn. Seaforth Highlanders
— JUNE 11th 1916 —

1. The 8th Seaforth Highlanders will relieve the 13th Royal Scots in the Right Sub-Section of the HULLUCH SECTOR on the 12th June, 1916.

2. "D" Coy. Seaforth Hights. will relieve the Rt. Coy. of the 13th Royal Scots
   "C" Coy.    "    "    "    Centre Coy. "    "    "
   "B" Coy.    "    "    "    Left Coy. "    "    "
   "A" Coy.    "    "    "    Support Coy. "    "    "

3. Companies will march to-morrow as follows.
   STARTING POINT ............... Guard Room Corner.
   TIME ........................... 7.15 a.m.
   ORDER of March ............... "D" Coy. and Hd. Qrs. Signallers, "C" Coy, "B" Coy and "A" Coy.
   ROUTE. SAILLY-LA-BOURSE — ANNEQUIN — VERMELLES CHURCH.
   Coys. will move off at 15 mins. interval.
   Guides, 1 per Platoon, will be at CHURCH VERMELLES, at 9 a.m.

4. All movements East of SAILLY-LA-BOURSE, will be by Platoons at 200 yds. intervals.

5. Advanced Parties will leave under 2/Lt. D.M. Cameron and will include the following:-
   (a) 1 N.C.O per Coy. to take over Trench Stores — Sgt. Scarff will take over for Headquarters.
   (b) 2/Lt. Cameron will take over all Snipers Posts.
   (c) 2/Lt. J.H. Ross will take over the duties of Sports Officer in Rt. Sub-Section and remain on this duty during the Brigade's tour in the Trenches.
   (d) All Lewis Guns.
   Guides for No 5, from 13th Bn. The Royal Scots, will be at the Church, VERMELLES, at 5 p.m. to-day.

6. One Company of the K.O.R. Lancs. Regt. will be attached to the Battalion as under:-
   1 Platoon to each Coy. with Coy. Head Quarters with our "A" Coy.

7. 1st Line Transport will move to NOYELLES at 10 a.m. and take over from 13th Royal Scots.

8. Packs and Officers Valises will be stored in Quartermasters stores by 6 a.m.
   The Transport Officer will make arrangements for transporting mess Boxes, dixchies etc, to be collected not later than 7 a.m.

(Cont'd)

(Operation Order Cont'd)

9. The Quartermaster will arrange to hand over the Assault Course at LABOURSE to the Billeting party of the 7th Royal Scots Fusiliers on their arrival this evening.

10. All Trench Store returns to be rendered to Battn. Headquarters by mid-day to-morrow.
  Map Ref. of Battn. Headquarters to be notified later.
  Coy. Commanders will report completion of Relief to Bn. Hd.Qrs. immediately.

S. J. Morrell. Lieut.,
a/Adjutant, 8th Seaforth Highlanders.

Issued at 11.30 a.m.

Copy. No. 1 – 'A' Coy.
" " 2 – 'B' Coy.
" " 3 – 'C' Coy.
" " 4 – 'D' Coy.
" " 5 – Machine Gun Officer.
" " 6 – Transport Officer
" " 7 – Quartermaster.
" " 8 – War Diary.
" " 9 – File.
" " 10 – 11th Battn. K.O.R. Lancs.

———~——— II ———~———

SECRET

War Diary

OPERATION ORDER No 2
- Lieut. Col. D. A. Thomson -
- Commdg. 8th Bn. Seaforth Highrs -
June 15th 1916

APPENDIX III

1. "B" Coy. of the 11th K.O.R. Lancs. Regt." will leave the Trenches and proceed to Rest Billets in SAILLY-LA-BOURSE on the 16th inst. via TENTH AVENUE, LERUTOIRE ALLEY, CHURCH VERMELLES, PHILOSOPHE X Roads -NOYELLES.

2. Time - No 5 Platoon of K.O.R. Lancs Regt. to pass VERMELLES CHURCH at 9.15 A.M followed by No.6, No.7, & No.8 platoons.
Movement from Trenches to SAILLY-LA-BOURSE will be by platoons at 200 yds. interval.
A Seaforth Guide per platoon will accompany the K.O.R. Lancs Regt. as far as the CHURCH, VERMELLES. These will be detailed by Officers Commanding Coys to which the platoons are attached.

3. The 8th Seaforth Highrs. will arrange to provide breakfasts for the out-going Coy. of the 11th K.O.R. Lancs. Regt. before leaving the Trenches.

4. Battalion Headquarters of the 11th K.O.R. Lancs. Regt. will move from BETHUNE to SAILLY-LA-BOURSE at on the afternoon of the 15th inst.

5. Billeting Party of the 11th K.O.R. Lancs. Regt. (1 N.C.O per Coy.) will rendezvous at the Battn. Quartermaster's Stores at HUSSAR ROAD, SAILLY-LA-BOURSE, at 5 p.m. on the 15th inst. These N.C.O will report to H.Q. 8th Seaforths at 2 p.m. on the 15th inst.

6. Capt. H. B. Johnstone, 7th Cameron Highrs., is appointed instructor during period 11th K.O.R. Lancs Regt. are in Rest. Billets. He will report to O.C. 11th K.O.R. Lancs. Regt. at 10.a.m on the 16th at Battn. Headquarters, SAILLY-LA-BOURSE.

S. Morrell
Lieut.,
o/Adjutant 8th Seaforth Highlanders.

# SECRET — OPERATION ORDER No 3

by
Lieut. Col. H. A. Thomson
Commdg. 8th (S) Battn. Seaforth Highrs.

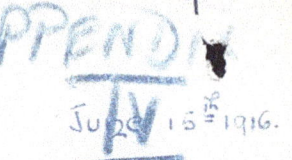

APPENDIX IV
June 15th 1916.

1. The 8th Battn. Seaforth Highrs. will be relieved by the 7th Cameron Highlanders to-morrow – 16th June.

2. Companies will be relieved in the following order:-
   - "B" Coy. Seaforth Highrs. will be relieved by "C" Coy. Cameron Highrs.
   - "D" Coy.      "        "         "      "    "D" Coy.    "       "
   - "C" Coy.      "        "         "      "    "B" Coy.    "       "
   - "A" Coy.      "        "         "      "    "A" Coy.    "       "

   Guides (1 per platoon) will be at junction of HAY ALLEY and TENTH AVENUE at 2:30 p.m. to guide incoming Companies of the 7th Cameron Highrs.
   Route for incoming Companies – HAY ALLEY

3. On relief, Coys. will move into Brigade Support as follows:-
   - "B" Coy. to O.B. 4 and 5 via WINGS WAY at present occupied by "B" Coy. Cameron Hrs.
   - "D" Coy. to TENTH AVENUE via VENDIN ALLEY    "      "      "   "D" Coy.    "    "
   - "C" Coy. to      "        via       "        "      "      "   "C" Coy.    "    "
   - "A" Coy. to CURLEY CRESCENT via    "         "      "      "   "A" Coy.    "    "

   "A" Coy. will not enter VENDIN ALLEY until "C" Coy. is clear of RESERVE LINE.

4. Advanced Parties of the 7th Cameron Hrs. will be at Junction of HAY ALLEY and 10th AVENUE at 2 p.m where they will be met by guides of the 8th Seaforth Highrs. as follows:-
   1 guide from "B" Coy. 8th Seaforth Hrs. (Bombers) to conduct bombers of "C" Coy. Cameron Highrs.
   1 guide per Coy. to conduct parties to take over Trench Stores.

5. Advanced Parties of the 8th Seaforth Highrs. consisting of 1 N.C.O + 1 man per Coy. will be at Coy. Headquarters 7th Cameron Highrs. at 10 a.m. to-morrow to take over Trench Stores, Dug-outs etc.
   The one man per Coy. proceeding with advanced parties will reconnoitre the Route and be responsible for guiding his Company to their new position on Relief.

6. Trench Stores will be handed over as arranged to-day between Coy. Commanders concerned. Receipts to be forwarded to Battn. H.Q. by 9 a.m. 17th inst.

7. Completion of Relief will be reported by wire to Battn. Hd.Qrs.

COPY No. 1 – O.C "A" Coy.
        2 – O.C "B"  "
        3 – O.C "C"  "
        4 – O.C "D"  "
        5 – O.C 7th Cameron Hrs.
        6 – Quartermaster
        7 – Transport Officer
        8 – War Diary.
        9 – File.

S. J. Morrell.
Lieut.
Adjutant 8th Seaforth Highlanders

SECRET

# OPERATION ORDER No. 4
### Lieut. Col. N. A. Thomson
### Commdg. 8th (S) Battn. Seaforth Highrs.

**APPENDIX V**

June 1916

1. The 8th Battn. Seaforth Highrs. will relieve the 8/10th Gordon Hrs. in the Left Sub-section, HULLUCH SECTION to-morrow, 20th June 1916.

2. Coys. will relieve in the following order:-
   - "B" Coy. 8th Seaforth Hrs. will relieve "D" Coy. 8/10th Gordon Hrs. in LEFT FIRING LINE.
   - "C" Coy. " " " " " "C" Coy. 8/10th " " " RIGHT " "
   - "A" Coy. " " " " " "B" Coy. " " " SUPPORT in O.G.I.
   - "D" Coy. " " " " " "A" Coy. " " " Reserve in O.B.I.

   Route for "B" Coy:- FOSSE WAY - GOEBEN ALLEY
   " " "C" Coy:- TENTH AVENUE, CHAPEL ALLEY
   " " "A" Coy:- CHAPEL ALLEY
   " " "D" Coy:- LE RUTOIRE ALLEY, O.B.I.

   Guides (1 per platoon) of 8/10th Gordon Hrs. for "B" and "C" Coys. will be at the junction of O.G.I. with FOSSE WAY and CHAPEL ALLEY respectively at 9.15 a.m. There will be no Guides for "A" and "D" Coys.

3. Advanced parties, consisting of 1 N.C.O and 1 man per Coy; 1 N.S.O for Headquarters; and the Bombing Officer, to take over trench stores, bomb-stores etc. will proceed to Coy. and Battalion Headquarters, respectively of 8/10th GORDON HIGHRS. at 7.30 a.m. to-morrow. Receipts of trench stores will be given and a copy forwarded to Battn. Hd. Qrs. by 9 a.m. 21st June.

4. Guards on water pump, Brigade Bomb Stores, Brigade Hd. Qrs, Chapel Keep and R.E dump (junction of Curley CRESCENT and HULLUCH ROAD) will remain until relieved by Guards of the 8/10th Gordon Hrs.

5. 2/Lieut. M. Jackson is detailed to check ammunition in the entire Left Sub-section. He will report to Battn. Hd. Qrs. as soon as possible after the relief is complete.

6. Completion of Reliefs will be reported by wire to Battn. Hd. Qrs.

---

COPY. No 1. OC. "A" Coy.
2. OC. "B" Coy.
3. OC. "C" Coy.
4. OC. "D" Coy.
5. OC. 8/10th Gordon Hrs.
6. Bombing Officer
7. Transport Officer
8. Quartermaster.
9. War Diary
10. File.

George W. Duncan
Lieut.,
Adjutant 8th Seaforth Hrs.

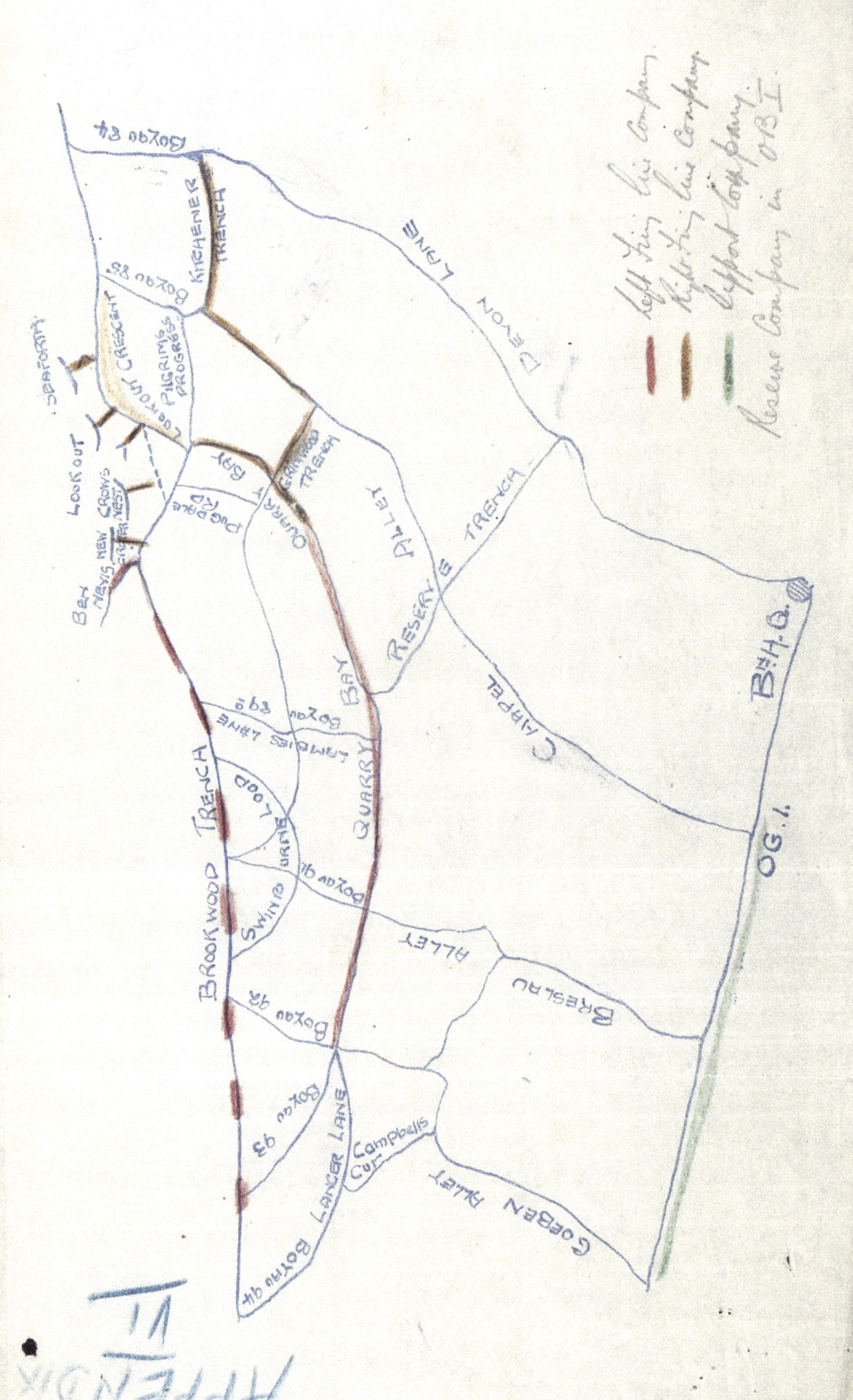

**SECRET**

**APPENDIX VII**

COPY No. 7

## OPERATION ORDER No. 5.

Lieut. Col. N. A. Thomson.
Commdg. 8th Battn. Seaforth Highrs.

June 19th 1916

1. "A" Coy. of the 13th East Surrey Regt. will leave the Trenches and proceed to Rest Billets SAILLY LABOURSE on the 20th inst. via LE RUTOIRE ALLEY; CHURCH, VERMELLES; CROSS ROADS, PHILOSOPHE; NOYELLES.

    No. 1 platoon will pass the Church, VERMELLES at 9.15 a.m. followed by Nos. 2, 3 and 4 platoons. Platoons will move at 200 yds. intervals.

---

2. The 8th Seaforth Hrs. will arrange to provide breakfasts for out-going Coy. of 13th East Surrey Regt.

---

3. I Coy. of the 11th K.O.R. Lancs. Regt. will be attached to the Battalion for Company training in the Front Line from 20th to 22nd inst. This Coy. will be met by 4 Seaforth Guides at Church VERMELLES, at 1.15 p.m. to-morrow, 20th inst. These Guides will be detailed by O.C. "D" Coy, and will bring this Coy. via CHAPEL ALLEY, to Junction of O.B.I and CHAPEL ALLEY; where they will be met by a second lot of guides who will take them to their position in the Trenches.

---

4. I Lewis Gun Team of the 11th K.O.R. Lancs. Regt. will be attached to the Battalion from 20th to 22nd inst. They will arrive at VERMELLES CHURCH at 12.15 p.m. where they will be met by a guide to be detailed by O.C. "D" Coy. They will then proceed via CHAPEL ALLEY to Junction of O.B.I with CHAPEL ALLEY where they will be met by a second guide who will conduct them to their position in the Trenches.

---

George B. Duncan.
Lieut,
Adjutant, 8th Seaforth Highlanders.

**Distribution.**

Copy. No. 1. - O.C. "A" Coy.
2. - O.C. "B" "
3. - O.C. "C" "
4. - O.C. "D" "
5. - O.C. "A" Coy. 13th East Surrey Regt.
6. - Transport Officer.
7. - War Diary
8. - File.

SECRET     OPERATION - ORDER Nº 6     COPY No 6

APPENDIX VIII

Lieut. Col. N. A. Thomson.
Commdg. 8th Battn. Seaforth Highrs.

June 20th 1916

(1.) "B" Coy, 11th K.O.R. Lancs. Regt. will relieve "C" Coy. 8th Seaforth Hrs. in Right firing line, Left Sub-Section, HULLUCH SECTION to-morrow 21st June 1916.

(2.) Route for "B" Coy., 11th K.O.R. Lancs. Regt, CHAPEL ALLEY.
Guides - (1 per platoon) from "C" Coy. 8th Seaforth Hrs. will be at junction of O.G.1 with CHAPEL ALLEY at 10 a.m. to-morrow.

(3.) O.C. "B" Coy. 11th K.O.R. Lancs. Regt, will arrange to visit line of "C" Coy. 8th Seaforth Hrs. at 6 a.m. to-morrow, 21st inst.

(4.) Advanced party of 1 Officer and 1 N.C.O. of "B" Coy. 11th K.O.R. Lancs. Regt, to take over Trench Stores will be at H.Q. "C" Coy. 8th Seaforth Hrs at 8 a.m. to-morrow. Receipts will be forwarded to Battn H.Q. by 4 p.m to-morrow, 21st inst.

(5.) O.C. "C" Coy. 8th Seaforth Hrs. will arrange to leave 1 Officer (2nd/Lieut. K. McKenzie) 1 Bombing Sergeant and 8 Bombers (2 for each sap) in Front Line. They will come under orders of O.C. "B" Coy. 11th K.O.R. Lancs. Regt. from time the relief is complete.

(6.) On relief, 2 platoons of "C" Coy. 8th Seaforth Hrs., will proceed via DEVON LANE to RESERVE TRENCH between CHAPEL ALLEY and DEVON LANE.
Remaining 2 Platoons of "C" Coy. 8th Seaforth Hrs. will proceed via DEVON LANE to O.G.1 between CHAPEL ALLEY and DEVON LANE.

(7.) Completion of Relief will be reported by runner to Battn. H.Q.

George W. Duncan
Lieut.,
Adjutant, 8th Seaforth Highlanders.

DISTRIBUTION

COPY. NO. 1   O.C. "B" Coy., 11th K.O.R. Lancs. Regt.
"   "   2   O.C. "C" Coy., 8th Seaforth Hrs.
"   "   3   O.C. "A" Coy. 8th Seaforth Hrs. } For Information
"   "   4   O.C. "B" Coy. 8th Seaforth Hrs. }
"   "   5   O.C. "D" Coy. 8th Seaforth Hrs.
"   "   6   WAR DIARY
        7   FILE

**SECRET** — **OPERATION ORDER No. 7.**

COPY No. 7

APPENDIX IX

Lieut. Col. N. A. Thomson
Commdg. 8th (S) Bn. Seaforth Highrs.

June 22nd 1916

1. "B" Coy. 11th K.O.R. Lancs. Regt. will be relieved in the right firing line, Right Sub-Section, HULLUCH SECTOR by a Coy. of 13th East Surrey Regt. to-morrow 23rd June 1916.

2. Guides (1 per platoon) 11th K.O.R. Lancs. Regt. and 1 per platoon "C" Coy. 8th Bn. Seaforth Highlanders will rendezvous at Battn. H.Q., 8th Seaforth Hrs., under an Officer to be detailed by O.C. "C" Coy. 8th Seaforth Hrs. at 8.30 a.m. 23rd June 1916. They will then proceed to church VERMELLES, where they will meet the incoming Company, 13th East Surrey Regt. at 9.45 a.m. and guide them via CHAPEL ALLEY to their position in the line.

3. On relief, "B" Coy. 11th K.O.R. Lancs. Regt. will proceed to rest billets at SAILLY LABOURSE via DEVON LANE, O.G.I, LE RUTOIRE ALLEY.

4. 1 Lewis Gun Team, 13th East Surrey Regt. will arrive at Church VERMELLES at 8.15 a.m, 23rd June, 1916, where they will be met by a guide to be detailed by O.C. "C" Coy, 8th Seaforth Hrs, who will guide the team to Battn. H.Q. 8th Seaforth Hrs, via CHAPEL ALLEY, and O.G.I.

5. All Trench Stores will be handed over and receipts forwarded to Battn. H.Q. 8th Seaforth Hrs., by 2 p.m, 23rd June, 1916.

6. Completion of Relief will be reported by runner to Battn. H.Q. 8th Battn. Seaforth Hrs.

7. During the tour of duty in the line of the Coy. of 13th East Surrey Regt. O.C. "C" Coy. will detail 1 Officer, 1 bombing Sgt., and 8 bombers to be attached to the Coy. of 13th East. Surrey Regt. as instructors.

George W. Duncan
Lieut.,
Adjutant. 8th Seaforth Highlanders.

DISTRIBUTION
Copy No. 1 — OC "B" Coy. 11th K.O.R. Lancs. Regt.
" No. 2 — OC "C" Coy. 8th Seaforth Hrs.
" No. 3 — OC "A" Coy. " " "  ⎫
" No. 4 — OC "B" Coy. " " "  ⎬ For Information.
" No. 5 — OC "D" Coy. " " "  ⎭
" No. 6 — Transport Officer " "
" No. 7 — War Diary
" No. 8 — FILE

SECRET
(1) O.C. "Trench Mortar Batty.") 8th Seaforth HS
(2) ~~Lewis Gun Officer~~
(3) FILE.

D.998

Appendix K

Ref. Trench Map 1/10,000

1/ Strong Patrols will go out simultaneously along the Division Front at 1.45 a.m. to-night 25/26th June, to ascertain the effects of LOOS WAILERS, capture prisoners, destroy material and obtain identifications.

2/ There are no LOOS WAILERS actually on our Battn. Front but there are some to the north and south of us.

3/ A patrol of 13th Royal Scots on our left will go out from BOYAU 94 and proceed from there until they reach point G.12.a.½.3¾; They will then enter the German line at a point G.12.a.0.4, and bomb back towards their own lines over the HAIRPIN CRATERS.

4/ A patrol of 8/10th Gordon HIS on our right will raid the German Front Line between about BOYAU 76(a),(H.13.a.1.7½) and BOYAU 79 (G.12.d.9.5). At 2 a.m. a bugler will sound the Cookhouse Call in Gordon Trenches to recall 8/10th Gordon's raiding parties.

5/ A small patrol of "A" Coy. 8th Seaforth HIS. will go out from between BOYAU 89 and 91 under special instructions issued to O.C. "A" Coy.

6. As part of the general operations, smoke candles and "P" bombs will be burnt between BRESLAU AVENUE and BOYAU 94 under arrangements to be made by O.C. "A" Coy in accordance with I Corps 854/22 G.19 d/13.6.16 which has been issued to him.

7. The following operations will precede the above raids:—
   1 a.m. – 1·15 a.m.  L.W's in action.
   1·10 a.m. – 1·15 a.m.  Smoke Candles.
   1·15 a.m. – 1·25 a.m.  Smoke with "P" bombs.
   1·10 a.m. – 1·20 a.m.  Intense Artillery [Bombardment]
   1·20 a.m. – 1·40 a.m.  Slow Continuous " "
   1·40 a.m. – 1·50 a.m.  Artillery lift and form barrages to assist patrols.

8. The Battn will stand to arms at 12·15 a.m. and will not stand down until orders are received from Battn H.Q.

9. In the event of heavy hostile shelling, the men will take cover in any dug-outs available in the trenches which they are then occupying. They must take their rifles with them and be ready for instant action. A double sentry will be posted at each entrance of dug-outs. One man will watch for hostile action and the other warn the occupants of the dug-outs. If either becomes a casualty he must be replaced at once.

10. All ranks will wear gas helmets as for Gas Alert.

11. 1 Officer per Coy. will remain at the telephone at Coy. H.Q.

12. A sharp look-out will be kept in case gas blows back from other parts of the line.

13. All watches will be set by Brigade Time which was notified to Coys at 5 p.m. to-day.

14. Acknowledge

~~~~~

June 25th 1916        George W Sm——
                   Lieut,
               Adjutant, 8th Seaforth His.

SECRET                                          COPY No...
## OPERATION ORDER                    APPENDIX
by                                                  XI
Lieut. Col. N.A. Thompson D.S.O.
Commdg. 8th Bn. Seaforth Highrs.     25.9.16

1. "B" Coy. 13th Scot. Surrey Regt. will relieve "D" Coy. 8th Seaforth Hrs. tomorrow 26th inst. at .......... time. Our Sub-Section H.Q. per SECTOR.

2. Guides (1 per platoon) from B Coy 13th Scot Surrey Regt. will be at junction of TUNNEL DULEY POSTS at 6.15 a.m. tomorrow 26th and will guide B Coy. to their position in the line.

3. The M.G.O. 8th Seaforth Hrs will arrange to relieve the guns of the Scot. Surrey Regt at 6 a.m. tomorrow.

4. Lewis gun all officers Lewis root m/g of inds. of B Coy Scot Surreys arrival be at Church VERMELLES at 9 a.m. tomorrow. There will be loaded on limbers and sent to Billets under arrangements to be made by Bustn. M.G.O.

5. On Relief "B" Coy. 13th Scot Surrey Regt. will move via BREWERY AVENUE, STAFFORD LANE, & .B.T. & .............. FIELD ROAD, to pass the Church, VERMELLES at 9.45 a.m. and will move thence to BETHUNE via CROSS ROADS L.6.K via SAILLY LA BOURSE - BEUVRY. Movement East of SAILLY LA BOURSE to be by platoons at 200 yds. interval.

6. After this Relief, O.C. "C" Coy. will withdraw 2 platoons from O.G.1. to O.G.1 + take over the area previously occupied by D Coy.

7. Completion of Relief to be reported by runner to Bustn. H.Q.
                    ~~~~
COPY No. 1  O.C.  C Coy  13th Scot Survey Regt.
        2. O.C.  D Coy.  8th Seaforth Hrs.        M......... Lieut.
        3. O.C.  C Coy.    do        Adjutant 8th Seaforth Highrs
        4. O.C.  B Coy.    do
        5. O.C.  A Coy.    do
        6. M.G.O.          do
        7  FILE
                    ~~~~

8th Seaforth H

S.E.C.R.E.T.

44th Brigade
B.M./32

All Battns. 44th Inf.Bde.
44th M.G.Coy.
44th T.M.Battery.
Brigade Transport Officer.
Staff Capt.

1. Herewith 3 copies of the programme for L.W's and smoke on night 25/26th June, for issue to Company Commanders in front trenches.

   These are not to be taken into the trenches before the night 25/26th, and in the event of postponement are to be returned to Brigade Headquarters for issue on another date.

2. The following is the allotment of smoke candles and "P" bombs:-

   RIGHT SUB-SECTION.  1200 yards.
      Smoke candles.
         4 per minute per 25 yards, i.e. 80 for 5 minutes
         for 100 yards, i.e.  80 x 12 =  960.
      "P" Bombs.
         1 per 25 yards per minute, i.e. 40 per 100 yards
         for 10 minutes, i.e. 40 x 12 =  480.

   CENTRE SUB-SECTION.     700 yards (from Pt.G.12.d.6.6. (BRECON SAP)
                                        to right of sub-section).
      Smoke Candles.   80 x 7 =   560.
      "P" Bombs.       40 x 7 =   280.

   LEFT SUB-SECTION.   300 yards (from G.12.c.2.2.(BRESLAU AVENUE) to
                                 left of sub-section).

      Smoke candles.   80 x 3 =   240.
      "P" Bombs.       40 x 3 =   120.

3. The above quantities will be drawn from the Brigade Grenade Store, VERMELLES, to-night by Battalions.

   Arrangements are being made by the Staff Captain for the Brigade Transport Officer to detail Transport where required.

   The Brigade Transport Officer will arrange with Battalion Qr.Mrs. to send above smoke bombs and candles to Battalion Ration Dumps after the rations to-night, where a special officer from each battalion with a carrying party will meet them.

   "P" Bombs are packed 12 in a box; each box can be carried by 1 man.
   Smoke candles are packed 25 in a box; each box can be carried by one man.

                                                    Major,
                                                Brigade Major,
24-6-16.                               44th Infantry Brigade.

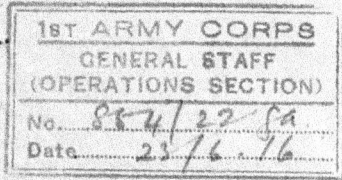

SECRET.

PROGRAMME OF L.W's AND SMOKE.

S E R I E S  "A".

    Concentrated L.W. attack at selected points followed by smoke along Corps front.

| | | |
|---|---|---|
| First night 25/26th June. | At 1:0 a.m. | 3 groups of 4 L.W's each - total 12 L.W's - to be discharged at full speed, simultaneously, ~~until exhausted~~. |
| | At 1:10 a.m. | Commence smoke cloud with smoke candles. |
| | At 1:15 a.m. | Turn off all cylinders. |
| | At 1:15 a.m. to 1:25 a.m. | Continue smoke cloud with "P" bombs. |

NOTE :-

1. Smoke Candles — Burn 4 candles per minute per 25 yards of front distributed evenly. Candles can be placed on the parapets.

2. "P" Bombs — Light and throw out as far as possible one bomb per minute per 25 yards of front; distribute along front evenly as far as possible.

-:-:-:-:-:-:-:-

Frontage of smoke.

    Whole Divisional front excluding
        G.12.d.6.6.(BRECON SAP) to G.12.c.2.8. (BRESLAU AVENUE)
        G. 5.d.3.0.(BORDER REDOUBT) to G.4.d.5.5.(Savile ROW)

S E C R E T.

I Corps 854/22 G.a. d/13-6-16.


PROGRAMME OF L.W's AND SMOKE.

S E R I E S "A".

Concentrated L.W. attack at selected points followed by smoke along Corps front.

| | | |
|---|---|---|
| First night 25/26th June. | At 1-0 A.M. | 3 groups of 4 L.W's each - total 12 L.W's - to be discharged at full speed, simultaneously. |
| | At 1-10 A.M. | Commence smoke cloud with smoke candles. |
| | At 1-15 A.M. | Turn off all cylinders. |
| | At 1-15 A.M. to 1-25 A.M. | Continue smoke cloud with "P" bombs. |

NOTE :-

1. <u>Smoke Candles</u> - Burn 4 candles per minute per 25 yards of front distributed evenly. Candles can be placed on the parapets.

2. <u>"P" Bombs</u> - Light and throw out as far as possible one bomb per minute per 25 yards of front; distribute along front evenly as far as possible.

-:-:-:-:-:-:-:-:-:-:-:-:-:-

Frontage of smoke.

Whole Divisional front excluding
G.12.d.6.6. (BRECON SAP) to G.12.c.9.8. (BRESLAU AVENUE).
G.5.d.3.0. (BORDER REDOUBT) to G.4.d.5.5. (SAVILE ROW).

SECRET.                                                              Copy No. 2

**44th Infantry Brigade Operation Order No.62.**

25-6-1916.

Reference Trench Map 1/10,000.

1. The hostile front line from G.12.d.6.8. to G.12.d.4½.8½. and the area enclosed by the circular trench joining these points will be raided on 27th June, 1916, with the object of –

   (i) Inflicting casualties.
   (ii) Destroying Machine Gun emplacements and damaging mine shafts.
   (iii) Securing prisoners.

2. The Artillery arrangements are shown in Appendix 'A'.

3. The raid will be carried out by 9th Black Watch in accordance with the following time table.-

   3-00 A.M. Hostile line on front of attack and elsewhere will be subjected to an intense bombardment (See Appendices 'A', 'B' and 'C'.)

   3-10 A.M. Raiding party will leave trenches and form up between BRECON SAP and MARSH CRATER.

   3-14 A.M. Smoke shells will be thrown on points G.12.d.7¾.7. G.12.d.2.9½. G.12.a.9.0½. G.12.a.3.0. if the wind is favourable.

   3-15 A.M. Raiding parties will rush the German trenches and Artillery will lift.

   3-35 A.M. Infantry will leave hostile trenches.

   3-40 A.M. Artillery will establish a barrage on enemy front line. (Or earlier if requested to do so).

   The details of the Infantry action are shown in Appendix 'D'.

4. The raiding party will be prepared to cut any wire that has not been cut by the trench mortars.

5. The word "Retire" will not be used, nor will any attention be paid to it.

6. A First Aid post will be established at the Mining Rescue Station in ARGYLL TRENCH.

7. All watches will be synchronised at Headquarters 9th Black Watch (FOSSE WAY) at MIDNIGHT 26th/27th June.

8. All prisoners will be sent to the special enclosure at West end of BREWERY VERMELLES, where they will be handed over to A.P.M., 15th Division. Their approximate numbers will be reported at earliest possible moment to Brigade Headquarters.

9. On conclusion of the operations all members of the raiding party will report to the Company H.Q. without delay.

( 2. )

10. The Brigade will "Stand to" at 3 A.M. and will not "Stand down" until ordered from Brigade H.Q.

In the event of heavy hostile shelling the men will take cover in any dug-outs available in the trenches which they are then occupying. They must take their rifles with them and be ready for instant action.
A double sentry will be posted at each entrance of dug-outs.- One man will watch for hostile action and the other warn the occupants of the dug-out. If either becomes a casualty he must be replaced at once.

11. Pass word "P E R T H".

Issued Through Signals

at 11 a.m.

*[signed]* Major,
Brigade Major,
44th Infantry Brigade.

Copies to :-

    No. 1. 9th Black Watch.
        2. 8th Seaforth Hrs.
        3. 8/10th Gordon Hrs.
        4. 7th Cameron Hrs.
        5. Right Group R.A.
        6. H.Q. 15th Division.
        7. File.

*Appendices issued only with copy to 15th Division*

S E C R E T.   **APPENDIX XIII**

All recipients of Operation Order No.9 dated 26th. June 1916.

1. Reference Operation Order No.9.d/ 26th. June 1916 para. 2 "A" Coy. will not now proceed to GOSNAY but will move to SAILLY LA BOURSE via GOEBEN ALLEY, FOSSE WAY, O.B.4., STANSFIELD ROAD, VERMELLES, CROSS ROADS L.6.c.

O.C. "A" Coy. will therefore arrange to send a billeting party in accordance with para. 3. to report at Quartermasters Stores NOYELLES at 3 p.m. 27th. June.

June 27th. 1916.

George W. Dunn
Lieut.
Adjutant 5th. Battalion Seaforth Highrs.

SECRET.                                                    Copy No. 10.

# OPERATION ORDER No. 9.
## by
### Lieut. Col. N.A.Thomson D.S.O.
### Commdg. 8th. Battn. Seaforth Highlanders.
### June 26th.1916

1.   The 8th. Seaforth Highlanders will be relieved by the 7/8th. K.O.S.B.s in the Left Sub-Section, HULLUCH SECTOR, on 28th. June 1916.

2.   Coys. will be relieved in the following order:-
"A" Coy. 8th. Seaforth Hrs. will be relieved by "C" Coy. K.O.S.B.s.
"D" Coy.        "         "        "        "        "       "D" Coy. K.O.S.B.s.
"B" Coy.        "         "        "        "        "       "A" Coy. K.O.S.B.s.
"C" Coy.        "         "        "        "        "       "B" Coy. K.O.S.B.s.
   Guides(1 per platoon) and 1 for Battn. H.Q. will be at Church VERMELLES,at 9 a.m. 28th. June to guide incoming Companies of the 7/8th. K.O.S.B.s.
   Route for incoming Coys. of the 7/8th. K.O.S.B.s CHAPEL ALLEY.
   On relief "A" Coy. will move via GOREEN ALLEY, FOSSE WAY, O.B.4., STANSFIELD ROAD,VERMELLES, to CROSS ROADS NOYELLES, where buses will meet them at 11 a.m. to take them to GOSNAY.
   "D" and "B" Coys. will move to SAILLY LA BOURSE via CHAPEL AVEN. O.B.1., FOSSE WAY, O.B.4., STANSFIELD ROAD,VERMELLES,CROSS ROADS, L.S.C.
   "C" Coy. will move to NOYELLES via FOSSE WAY,O.B.4., STANSFIELD ROAD,and VERMELLES.
   All movements East of SAILLY LA BOURSE will be by platoons at 200 yards interval.

3.   Billeting Parties (4 per Coy. except for "A" Coy. and 1 for Headquarters) will report at Quartermasters Stores NOYELLES,at 5 p.m. on the 27th. June and will proceed under 2/Lieut. A.M.Miller to take over Billets from the 12th .H.L.I. at SAILLY LA BURSE and NOYELLES respectively.

4.   Lewis Guns will be relieved on the 27th. June 1916. 1 guide per Lewis Gun will be sent to the Brewery VERMELLES,at 2 p.m.27th.inst.
   On relief Lewis Gun detachment will move to SAILLY LA BOURSE and report to Headquarters 12th. H.L.I.

5.A.   Advanced Parties of the 7/8th. K.O.S.B.s as under will arrive at Church VERMELLES at 5 p.m. 27th. June where they will be met by 1 guide per Coy. and 1 for Headquarters.
   1 Officer per Battn. and 1 N.C.O. per Coy.to take over trench Stores.
   Battalion Bombing Officer.
   Battalion Sniping and Intelligence Officer.
   1 N.C.O. to take over Advanced Bomb Store in O.B.1. between DEVON LANE and CHAPEL ALLEY.

6.   Carrying Parties for Tunnelling CCoys. up to and including reliefs going on duty at 10 a.m.(which will be relieved at 4 p.m.) will be found by "C" Coy. as usual on 28th. inst.. These Parties will be marched to their Billets on relief by their respective Commanders.

7.   First Line Transport will move to BETHUNE under arrangements to be made by the Transport Officer.

8.   All surplus Kit and Mess Boxes will be sent down with Ration Trolleys to-morrow night 27th. June.

(Continued)

9. All Dixchies and remaining Mess Kit will be sent down at 7 a.m. on the 28th. June to Brewery VERMELLES where three limbers to be detailed by the Transport Officer will meet them at 8 a.m.

10. Receipts will be taken for Trench Stores and rendered to Battalion Headquarters by 6 p.m. 29th. June.

11. Completion of Relief to be reported to Battalion H.Q..

George W. Duncan.
Lieut.,
Adjutant 8th. Bn. Seaforth Highlanders.

DISTRIBUTION.

Copy No...1...O.C. "A" Coy.
         2...O.C. "B" Coy.
         3...O.C. "C" Coy.
         4...O.C. "D" Coy.
         5...M.G.O.
         6...Transport Officer.
         7...Quartermaster.
         8...O.C. 7/8th. K.O.S.B.s.
         9...2/Lieut. A.J.M.Miller.
        10...War Diary.
        11...File.

## CONFIDENTIAL.

## WAR DIARY

of.

8th (Service) Battalion Seaforth Highlanders

From 1st July, 1916.   To 31st July, 1916.

(Volume 13.)

In the Field
31-7-1916.

Wm Thomson.
Lt. Colonel
Comdt. 8th Bn Seaforth Highlanders

Army Form C. 2118.

# WAR DIARY
# or
# INTELLIGENCE SUMMARY.
*(Erase heading not required.)*

Instructions regarding War Diaries and Intelligence Summaries are contained in F. S. Regs., Part II. and the Staff Manual respectively. Title pages will be prepared in manuscript.

| Place | Date | Hour | Summary of Events and Information | Remarks and references to Appendices |
|---|---|---|---|---|
| Sailly LA Bourse | 1/7/16 | | Battalion in billets - Training was carried on under Company arrangements, including Handling of Arms, Gas helmet drill & bayonet fighting. Battalion Horses trained under Lieut. J. M. McCallum. - A Draft of 42 O.R. joined the Bn. this day. | [init.] |
| Sailly LA Bourse | 2/7/16 | 9 am 12 noon | All gas helmets were inspected by the Divisional Gas Officer. CHURCH PARADE Ordered Divisional Recreation Room. 2/Lieut. J.M.L. Nicholson joined for duty. | [init.] |
| Sailly LA Bourse | 3/7/16 | | Battalion in billets - Training carried on under Company arrangements. Working parts of 4 officers & 150 men supplied by the Battalion for McCrorrors & 45th Infantry Brigs. | [init.] |
| Sailly LA Bourse | 4/7/16 | | Battalion in billets - Training as above including training of Lewis Gun Teams, bombers, &c. Lieut R.P. Smith joined for duty today. | [init.] |
| Sailly LA Bourse | 5/7/16 | | Battalion in billets - Training as above. Lieut T.M. Darling struck off the Strength of the Battalion - Capt C.C. Forsyth having been transferred to R.A.M.C. is struck off the Strength from today. | [init.] |

Army Form C. 2118.

# WAR DIARY
or
## INTELLIGENCE SUMMARY.
(Erase heading not required.)

Instructions regarding War Diaries and Intelligence Summaries are contained in F. S. Regs., Part II. and the Staff Manual respectively. Title pages will be prepared in manuscript.

| Place | Date | Hour | Summary of Events and Information | Remarks and references to Appendices |
|---|---|---|---|---|
| SAILLY LABOURSE BDE SUPPORT HOHENZOLLERN SECTION | 6/7/16 | — | The Battn this day relieved the 6th Battn Cameron Highlanders as per attached Operation Order No1. Relief was completed at 1.40pm. The whole Battalion was employed during the night on working & carrying parties for tunnelling companies & 174th Field Coy RE. Lieut S.J. MORRELL was this day wounded in action. Lieut A.C. Duncan M.O. admitted to hospital. Defence Scheme attached. | Appendix I Appendix II Appendix III |
| BDE SUPPORT HOHENZOLLERN SECTION | 7/7/16 | | A quiet day. Nothing to report. Working & carrying parties found as before. | ford. |
| BDE SUPPORT HOHENZOLLERN SECTION | 8/7/16 | | A quiet day. At 9.50pm the Battalion was ordered to "Stand-to" owing to an enemy attack on the Right Brigade of the Division. At 10pm orders were received to send 4 platoons & 2 Lewis Guns to O.G.I between the ATTUCK ROAD & CHAPEL ALLEY to come under the orders of O.C. 10th/11th H.L.I. This Order was Cancelled 5 minutes after being received. Stand down was ordered at 10.20pm. | ford |
| BDE SUPPORT HOHENZOLLERN | 9/7/16 | | A quiet day - nothing to report. | ford |

# WAR DIARY or INTELLIGENCE SUMMARY

Army Form C. 2118.

(Erase heading not required.)

Instructions regarding War Diaries and Intelligence Summaries are contained in F.S. Regs., Part II. and the Staff Manual respectively. Title pages will be prepared in manuscript.

| Place | Date | Hour | Summary of Events and Information | Remarks and references to Appendices |
|---|---|---|---|---|
| BDE SUPPORT HOHENZOLLERN SECTION | 10/1/16. | | "A" & "D" Coys relieved "C" & "D" Coys 7th Cameron High'rs in accordance with Operation Ord. No 2. 2 Coys took over of O.C. 7th Cameron High'rs. a relief was completed at 10.45 P.M. During the night of 10th/11th July a raid was carried out by "B" & "C" Companies under the Command of Major G.R. Jameson in accordance with Operation Order No.1. The operation was successfully carried out but report attached. Our Casualties were - Killed - 6 O.R. Wounded - 6 Officers (CAPT.F.HOLMES, CAPT F.G.HART, LIEUT J.E.SMITH, LIEUT F.M. McCALLION, LIEUT K. MCKENZIE, LIEUT A.J.M.MILLER) + 57 O.R. Much damage was done to the German Trenches & an OFFIZIER-ASPIRANT & 1 O.R. Captured & brought back to our lines - He belonged to the 23rd BAVARIAN REGT. | Appendix IV. Appendix V. Appendix VI |
| BDE SUPPORT HOHENZOLLERN SECTION | 11/1/16. | | "B" & "C" Coys relieved "A" & "B" Coys 7th Cameron High'rs in accordance with Operation Ord. No 3. Owing to the heaviness of bombarding "B" & "C" Coys after the raid & the previous night the relief was postponed until 2 p.m. It was found necessary owing to the weak strength of "B" Coy to place one platoon of "C" Coy under orders of O.C. "B" Coy. Also further to extend the front held by "A" & "D" Coys the Platoon that of "B" Coy. Sketch showing disposition of Companies attached. | Appendix VII Appendix VIII |

# WAR DIARY
## or
## INTELLIGENCE SUMMARY.
*(Erase heading not required.)*

Army Form C. 2118.

| Place | Date | Hour | Summary of Events and Information | Remarks and references to Appendices |
|---|---|---|---|---|
| LEFT SUB SECTION HOHENZOLLERN SECTION | 11/7/16 | 5.15 am | 2nd Lieut. T.M.L. NICHOLSON was killed in action by a hi-explosive shell. | |
| | | | Capt. I.H.S. JAMIESON joined for duty. He may shortly take Command of "D" Coy. | |
| | | | Lieut. A.W. TURNBULL again Commands "B" Coy. vice Capt. F. HOLMES wounded. | |
| | | | Lieut D.B. MACAULAY now Commands "C" Coy. vice Capt. F.G. HART wounded. | Appendix IX. |
| | | | DEFENCE SCHEME for the Subsection attached. | |
| | | | The day & night passed quietly. | |
| LEFT SUB SECTION HOHENZOLLERN SECTION | 12/7/16 | | Enemy trench Mortars were active during the morning on our front & support lines. | |
| | | | Enemy Aircraft active especially opposite Russian Sap. | Ref. Jamieson |
| | | | Our Lewis Guns fired 4500 rounds harassing enemy Parapet in G.4.b. | 14000. |
| | | | Our Stokes Mortars fired 50 rounds - various targets in enemy front & support trenches - no retaliation by enemy. | |
| LEFT SUB SECTION HOHENZOLLERN SECTION | 13/7/16 | | Enemy very quiet - little activity on either side except for enemy snipers who were again active. Work was done on front & support lines & on GUILDFORD TRENCH (Bryan 113) - Saps were also worked on & deepened. | |
| | | 11.30pm | Listening patrols went out from STICKY TRENCH - the Enemy were heard working in his front line | |

**WAR DIARY**
or
**INTELLIGENCE SUMMARY.**
(Erase heading not required.)

Army Form C. 2118.

| Place | Date | Hour | Summary of Events and Information | Remarks and references to Appendices |
|---|---|---|---|---|
| LEFT SUBSECTION HOHENZOLLERN SECTION. | 13/4/16 | - | (1) An enemy patrol was encountered. | fut |
| LEFT SUBSECTION HOHENZOLLERN SECTION. | 14/4/16 | - | After the first day with the exception of being heavy trench mortars - we retaliated with Stokes Mortars & Our artillery fired on suspected enemy emplacements but with little effect. Enemy snipers again active. Our Lewis Guns fired 650 rounds during the night traversing enemy front line. Listening patrols go out last night. | fut |
| LEFT SUBSECTION HOHENZOLLERN SECTION | 15/4/16 | - | Enemy trench mortars again being active - retaliation quite unsatisfactory, it takes a considerable time to get into touch with the Howitzers - a direct wire is being laid from Batt. Headquarters to the Howitzer Batty. (D/71st Bgde) which is covering our front. Our snipers were active & claim 6 hits opposite Russian SAP. Our bombers were also active. Our enemy Sniperscope was out as also a few bombs fired from the Cup attachment. Listening patrols were out as on two previous nights. Our Lewis Guns fired 400 rounds during the night. | fut |

Army Form C. 2118.

# WAR DIARY
or
## INTELLIGENCE SUMMARY.
(Erase heading not required.)

Instructions regarding War Diaries and Intelligence Summaries are contained in F.S. Regs., Part II. and the Staff Manual respectively. Title pages will be prepared in manuscript.

| Place | Date | Hour | Summary of Events and Information | Remarks and references to Appendices |
|---|---|---|---|---|
| LEFT SUB-SECTION HOHENZOLLERN SECTION | 16/4/16 | | "C" Coy relieved "B" Coy in accordance with Order attached. Relief was completed by 8.55 A.m. | Appendix X |
| | | | Nothing unusual to report - Work was carried on repairing front & support trenches - these trenches are blown in daily by enemy heavy trench mortars. | |
| | | | Our artillery were very active between 11 am & 3.30 pm - the enemy did not retaliate not at all. | |
| | | | LIEUT A.J. TAYLOR, LIEUT R/B. MR. K. ROBERTSON & 10 O.R. having been invalided to the U.K. were struck off the strength of the battalion. | |
| LEFT SUB-SECTION HOHENZOLLERN SECTION | 17/4/16 | | Our artillery was again active during morning & afternoon. | |
| | | | Our Lewis Guns fired 1200 rounds during the night. | |
| | | 9.40 pm | Message received from O.C. "A" Coy. stating that it was thought possible that a relief has taken place in the enemy trenches as they appeared to be much friendlier. | Appendix VI |
| | | | Lewis Guns fired 1200 rounds during the night. | |
| | | | Nothing further to report. | |
| LEFT SUB-SECTION HOHENZOLLERN SECTION | 18/4/16 | 2 am | At this hour a party of men of the enemy attacked our new sap off Russian Left with bombs, our bombers drove the enemy left. Before he had time to throw a bomb, 1 Officer, one N.C.O fire took being — the enemy | |

# WAR DIARY
## or
## INTELLIGENCE SUMMARY.

*(Erase heading not required.)*

Army Form C. 2118.

Instructions regarding War Diaries and Intelligence Summaries are contained in F. S. Regs., Part II. and the Staff Manual respectively. Title pages will be prepared in manuscript.

| Place | Date | Hour | Summary of Events and Information | Remarks and references to Appendices |
|---|---|---|---|---|
| LEFT SUBSECTION HOHENZOLLERN SECTION | 18/4/16 | | Retaliated whereupon our forbes mortars opened very quickly. This brought out one of the enemy trench mortars. The enemy had 2 killed & 2 wounded. The casualties were two men wounded. The day was quiet. | |
| | | 11.30pm | Enemy discovered working on his horse about G.4.b.3½.7 & were dispersed by M. Lewis Gun fire. Lieut H. J. KIRKPATRICK was wounded in action today. | |
| LEFT SUBSECTION HOHENZOLLERN SECTION | 19/4/16 | | In Summary of operations see report attached. Retaliation to enemy heavy trench mortar was much more successful, both howitzers & our heavy trench mortar. | Appendix XII Appendix XIII |
| LEFT SUBSECTION HOHENZOLLERN SECTION | 20/4/16 | | In Summary of operations see report attached. | Appendix XIII |
| LEFT SUBSECTION HOHENZOLLERN SECTION | 21/4/16 | | In Summary of operations see report attached. Nothing further to report. | Appendix XIV |

# WAR DIARY
## or
## INTELLIGENCE SUMMARY.
*(Erase heading not required.)*

Army Form C.2118.

| Place | Date | Hour | Summary of Events and Information | Remarks and references to Appendices |
|---|---|---|---|---|
| LEFT SUB SECTION HOHENZOLLERN SECTION. | 22/9/16 | | The Battn. was this day relieved by the 2nd Battn. Rifle Brigade in accordance with attached Operation Order No.4. Relief was complete at 11.45 a.m. & the Battalion moved to Noeux-Les-Mines. | Appendix XV. |
| NOEUX LES MINES. | | | | Appx XVI |
| NOEUX LES MINES. | 23/9/16 | | The Battn. marched from Noeux to Ourton in accordance with Operation Order No.5 attached. The Battn. was in billets by 2 p.m. | Appendix XVI. Ibid. |
| OURTON. | | | | |
| OURTON. | 24/9/16 | | The day has devoted to general cleaning up & kit inspection under Company Arrangements. No.7045 L/Cpl. J. Hogg. awarded military medal by Commander in Chief under authority granted by His Majesty the King. | Ibid. |
| OURTON. | 25/9/16 | | Training was carried out as per attached order. Special attention was paid to the Training of Section Commanders. The following officers Joined for duty. 23rd inst. & were posted to companies as under :- Lieut. A. McADIE "B" Coy. Lieut. A.E. PARK "A" Coy. Major E.M. FRASER "C" Coy. Lieut. R.A. BERRY-HART "D" Coy. Lieut. T.R.R. TODD "C" Coy. | Appendix XVIII Ibid. Ibid. |
| OURTON. | 26/9/16 | | The Battalion marched from Ourton to AYEN DRIGNI as per attached operation order march table. arrived in new billets at 10.30 a.m. | Appendix XIX Ibid. |

# WAR DIARY
## or
## INTELLIGENCE SUMMARY
(Erase heading not required.)

Army Form C. 2118.

| Place | Date | Hour | Summary of Events and Information | Remarks and references to Appendices |
|---|---|---|---|---|
| AVESNOIGHT | 24/4/18 | | The Battalion marched from Avesnoignt to Barly as per attached operation order march tables attached Appendix IX. | |
| | | | Route via Crouy-en-Ternois - Hautin, Honval - Canteleux. | |
| | | | Battn. in billets by 2pm. | |
| | | | The Coy Commanders made authority granted by His Majesty the King awarded the Military Medal to the following:- No S/3645 Pte Alexander, No S/9302 Pte Enright, No S/6268 L/Cpl R.Emmett, No S/3302 L/Cpl M. Coleman, No 15483 Pte D. Stoddart (A/Camerons att 6th Seaforths), No S/9341 Pte H. Lowe, No S/8863 Pte T. Johnstone. | |
| | | | Capt. F. Holmes, 2nd Lieut F. McCallion & 450 OR having been invalided to United Kingdom the Strength of the Battn. reduced accordingly. | |
| BARLY | 25/4/18 | | The Battalion marched from Barly to Gezaincourt in accordance with operation order & march table attached. Route via Occoches, Hem. | Appendix X |
| | | | Battn. in billets by 10-30 am. | |
| | | | Following officers joined today - Lieut D.E.F.C. Hervey posted to "D" Coy. 2/Lieut N.N. Ritchie posted to "C" Coy. | NW |

Army Form C. 2118.

# WAR DIARY
## or
## INTELLIGENCE SUMMARY.
(Erase heading not required.)

Instructions regarding War Diaries and Intelligence Summaries are contained in F. S. Regs., Part II. and the Staff Manual respectively. Title pages will be prepared in manuscript.

| Place | Date | Hour | Summary of Events and Information | Remarks and references to Appendices |
|---|---|---|---|---|
| GEZAINCOURT | 29/4/16 | | Training was carried on under Company Arrangements, including training of Lewis Gunners. Special attention was paid to Rapid Loading, Description of Targets, Fire Orders. The Commanding Officer lectured to Company, Platoon & Section Commanders of "C" & "D" Coys. A draft of 50 O.R. joined the Battalion today. Attached training Order received from Bde H.Q. T.B. | Appendix XXI |
| GEZAINCOURT | 30/4/16 | | Church parade was held during the morning. In the afternoon - training was carried on. The Commanding Officer lectured to Company Platoon & Section Commanders of "A" & "B" Coys. | Appendix XXII |
| GEZAINCOURT | 2/5/16 | | The Battalion marched from Gezaincourt to Naours to Rendezvous with Aachen. March in order of march table. Battalion arrived in billets at 8 a.m. The General Officer Commanding in Chief under authority granted by His Majesty the King awarded to the following decorations. Lieut F.M. McCallion - Military Cross No. 5/8901 Pte. M Barrie - D.C.M. | Appendix XXIII |

# WAR DIARY
## or
## INTELLIGENCE SUMMARY.

Army Form C. 2118.

| Place | Date | Hour | Summary of Events and Information | Remarks and references to Appendices |
|---|---|---|---|---|
| M.A. Ctr. R.S. | 31/7/16 | | Lieut. W.P. McGavin reports for duty from hospital today. | Appendix XVIII |
| | | | Attached nominal roll received from 44th I.B. | Appendix XIX |
| | | | Attached Appendix XXIV showing Casualties from 1st July to 31st July 1916. | Appendix XXIV |

**S E C R E T.**    **O P E R A T I O N  O R D E R  No. 1.**    Copy No. 11

by

Lieut. Col. H.A. Thomson, D.S.O.,
Commanding 8th. Battalion Seaforth Highlanders
----------oOo----------

July 5th.

1. The 8th. Battn. Seaforth Hrs. will relieve the 6th. Battn. Cameron Hrs. in Brigade Support HOHENZOLLERN SECTION to-morrow 6th. July, 1916.

2. Companies will be relieved in the following order:-
   "D" Coy. 8th. Seaforth Hrs. will relieve "A" Coy. 6th. Cameron Hrs., in RAILWAY RESERVE TRENCH with 1 Platoon in CENTRAL KEEP.
   "A" Coy. 8th. Seaforth Hrs. will relieve "C" Coy. 6th. Cameron Hrs. in LANCASHIRE TRENCH with 1 Platoon in JUNCTION KEEP.
   "B" Coy. 8th. Seaforth Hrs. will relieve "B" Coy. 6th. Cameron Hrs. in LANCASHIRE TRENCH.
   "C" Coy. 8th. Seaforth Hrs. will relieve "D" Coy. 6th. Cameron Hrs. in LANCASHIRE TRENCH.
   Route for "D" Coy.- CROSS ROADS, Pt. L.6.c.-VERMELLES, QUARRY ALLEY.
   Route for "A" & "B" Coys.- CROSS ROADS, Pt. L.6.c.,-VERMELLES, to LANCASHIRE TRENCH- 1 Platoon of "A" Coy. to JUNCTION KEEP via HULLUCH ALLEY.
   Route for "C" Coy. NOYELLES, VERMELLES, to LANCASHIRE TRENCH.
   "D" Coy. will pass CROSS ROADS, SAILLY LABOURSE, at 11 a.m. (interval)
   All movement East of SAILLY LABOURSE will be by Platoons at 200yds.
   Guides (4 per Coy.) from 6th. Cameron Hrs. will be at CLARKES KEEP, at 12 noon.
   One Lewis Gun and Team will move with each Company.
   One Lewis Gun and Team will remain with Headquarters.

3. "A" Coy. will take over Brigade Headquarters Guard of 1 N.C.O. & 3 men.
   The Bombing Officer, 2/Lieut. A.J.M. Hilber, and 1 N.C.O., to be detailed by O.C. "A" Coy. will take over Brigade Bomb Store at CLARKES KEEP.

4. "A" "B" and "D" Coys. will stack all Packs and Surplus Mess Kit which is not being taken to the trenches at Quartermasters Stores by 6.30 a.m. to-morrow, 6th. inst. 2 Wagons for Packs and Valises etc. of "C" Coy. will be at Headquarters "C" Coy., NOYELLES, at 6.30 a.m. Officers Valises will be stacked at Quartermasters Stores at 9.30 a.m. All dixchies and Mess boxes which are being taken to the trenches will be stacked at the Coys. Cokers by 10 a.m. to-morrow, 6th. inst.- 1 limber per Company will be detailed to transport these to BREWERY VERMELLES.
   Headquarters Mess Cart will be at Headquarters Mess at 10 a.m.
   1 Limber for Orderly Room Stuff and Signalling Gear will be at Battn. Orderly Room at 10 a.m.

5. All Billets will be left scrupulously clean. O.C. Coys. will each detail one Officer to inspect all Billets after their Coys. have vacated them.

6. Transport will move from BETHUNE to SAILLY LABOURSE.

7. All Trench Stores will be handed over and receipts taken and forwarded to Battn. Headquarters by 6 p.m. 6th. July.

8. Completion of Reliefs will be reported by runner to Battn. Headquarters.

George W. Duncan.
Lieut.,
Adjutant 8th. Battalion Seaforth Highlanders.

DISTRIBUTION.
Copy. No. 1 Commanding Officer.    7. Machine Gun Officer.
         2. 2nd. in Command.         8. Transport Officer.
         3 O.C. "A" Coy.            9. Bombing Officer.
         4. O.C. "B" Coy.           10. O.C. 6th. Cameron Hrs.
         5 O.C. "C" Coy.            11. War Diary.
         6 O.C. "D" Coy.            12. File.

SECRET

# DEFENCE — SCHEME
## — LEFT-SUB-SECTION — HOHENZOLLERN SECTION —
### IX — 11th July 1916.

1. **BOUNDARIES OF SUB-SECTION.**

    (a) <u>Front Line</u> (including Crater System & Sap.)
    BOYAU 109 (exclusive) to MUD ALLEY (G.4.a.5.8.) inclusive.

    (b) <u>Support Line</u>. NORTHAMPTON TRENCH — from BOYAU 109 (exclusive) to Pt. G.4.a.9.7½.

    (c) <u>RESERVE LINE</u>. RESERVE TRENCH from Pt. G.10.a.8.7 to Pt. G.3.b.9½.1½.

2. <u>GARRISON</u> (a) — INFANTRY

    Front Line & Crater System and Support Line
    {
    From Boyau 109 (exclusive) to Boyau 110 (exclusive) — RIGHT COY.
    From Boyau 110 (inclusive) to Boyau 113 (exclusive) — CENTRE COY.
    From Boyau 113 (inclusive) to MUD ALLEY (inclusive) Pt. G.4.a.8.8 — LEFT COY.
    }

    <u>RESERVE LINE</u> — RESERVE TRENCH from Pt. G.10.a.8.7 to Pt. G.3.b.9½.1½ — RESERVE COY. less 1 platoon.
    1 Platoon in the QUARRY. Pt. G.4.a.5.3.

    (b) <u>In the event of an attack:</u> — or threatened attack the personnel of Tunnelling Corps and Infantry working with them will act as follows, coming under orders of the O.C. Corps. concerned.

    (1) <u>No.1 Section – 170th Tunnelling Coy.</u>

    <u>Infantry</u> will man the parapet of STICKY TRENCH between QUARRY ALLEY and RUSSIAN SAP. Relief attached Infantry in the QUARRY will man the parapet of NORTHAMPTON TRENCH on each side of Guildford TRENCH. Approx. strength in STICKY TRENCH — 20 Rifles — approx. strength in QUARRY — 40 Rifles.

    <u>R.E.</u> form a Bomb-carrying chain down LEFT BOYAU to join up with the chain formed up QUARRY ALLEY by the relief R.E. in the QUARRY.

        approx. Strength in STICKY TRENCH — 10
               "    "    " QUARRY    — 20

    (2) <u>No.4 Section – 170th (T) Coy. R.E.</u>

    <u>Infantry</u> — man the Parapet in NORTHAMPTON TRENCH on each side of BARTS ALLEY.
        approx. strength — 20 Rifles

    <u>R.E.</u> — Form a Bomb-carrying chain from NORTHAMPTON TRENCH up CORK STREET towards CRATER 4.
        approx. Strength — 10.

    (3) <u>No.3 Section – 170th (T) Coy. R.E.</u>

    <u>Infantry</u> — man the parapet of NORTHAMPTON TRENCH with their right on SAVILLE ROW.   approx. strength — 20 Rifles.

    <u>R.E.</u> act under orders of O.C. Centre-sub-section.

    NOTE. This section works mainly in the Centre-Sub-Section and except in the case of an attack is not included in the Garrison of Left-Sub-section.

3. <u>GENERAL PRINCIPLES OF DEFENCE:</u>

    (a) <u>First Line</u> to be held at all costs, and it is the duty of every Commander on the spot to counter attack should the line be broken.
    (b) <u>Support Line</u> is never to be left vacant.
    (c) Troops will never fall back from any one line to another, but all points will be defended whether their flanks are turned or not.

(cont'd)

## ACTION IN CASE OF ATTACK

(a) Outlying pickets will be warned by bugle, or if any of our own telephone or by firing three shots in rapid succession from any of outpost communication as well as by discharge of a rocket. These pickets will approach to [illegible] men will be with at day end.

(b) Commander of Reserve Coy. Support Coys and Companies of the Bn. in Reserve will at once come outside and be [illegible] out to [illegible] and keep themselves posted as to the situation. Battn. HQ will have Bde. H.Q. informed by telephone or runner.

(c) Should the enemy succeed in penetrating our defences [illegible] holding will be prepared to counter attack under orders of the O/C. Battn. it may be necessary to attack before the O/C. [illegible] this more important in case of emergency.

(d) If the front of the Brigade in our Bde. is penetrated a [illegible] line will be formed by 2 platoons of the Reserve Coy. along HUD BLEY. Remaining Bquad. of Reinforcement Coys will move along the front line and the line towers.

(e) O.C. Coys are responsible for withdrawing all men working in [illegible] in their area in the event of an enemy attack & if there are instructions of the Coy. may [illegible] such an attack, O.C. Coys will report to Battn. HQ [illegible] such actions taken.

## 5. Bombing Posts and Stores — as established on [illegible] on attached apparatus.

## 6. O.C. Firing Line Coys will make themselves acquainted with the positions of Bomb Stores in Support Trench. They will also make arrangements that parties are told off to carry bombs from the [illegible] line to where they may be wanted in Reinforcements and to parties those wants.

O.C. Reserve Coy. will tell off Parties to carry from Reserve Trench Bomb Stores to Support Line.

[illegible] (Reserve) [illegible] and Coys will carry from SUMMIT work to Support Line.

## 7. SPECIAL INSTRUCTIONS:

(a) [illegible] The Code signals to denote retake by our is "P.B.I. DAS" followed by Coy reporting. Troops will advance but on that [illegible] [illegible] and at sight of white contact [illegible] [illegible] be advanced order but [illegible] to man the Trenches.

A STRONG bell horn will be sounded at Brigade and attached unit at the directly a Gas attack is reported. As soon as a cloud has passed [illegible] Battn. will recover at once to Battn. H.Q. the condition of [illegible] [illegible] is which they work. [illegible] [illegible] as to [illegible] [illegible] [illegible] [illegible] [illegible] [illegible] Buzzer in (b). In the event of a Gas attack all men of the [illegible] [illegible] that in [illegible] should be placed from [illegible] to [illegible] [illegible] [illegible] [illegible] to be taken.

O.C. [illegible] Coys is responsible for warning Officers of [illegible] the buttery [illegible] [illegible] [illegible] [illegible] [illegible] [illegible] [illegible] [illegible] of the Buttery.

[illegible] [illegible] responsible for warning officers of the [illegible] [illegible] [illegible] the [illegible] and approved coast [illegible] to a [illegible] [illegible] [illegible].

(b) **FLAMMENWERFER:-** On the event of an attack by FLAMMENWERFER all troops in the Front Line Trenches will remain there. They will lie at the bottom of the trench. Troops on the Support line will man the parapet and open rapid fire and machine gun fire in the direction of the attack.

(c) **MINE.** If an enemy mine is exploded, as a general rule, the rear lip of the Crater will be occupied by digging a trench round it, with a connecting trench to the main line from either flanks.
   The procedure will be as follows:-
   A Bombing Squad will at once occupy the rear lip of the Crater pushing out a Bombing Post on each flank.
   The remainder of the Squad will dig themselves in, in the arc of the near lip. This action is to be taken before commencing to sap out to the Crater. The sap from fire trench to Crater will be commenced as soon as we are in possession of the near lip.
   Four Shovels per Bombing Squad will be kept where they will be available to be taken forward at once.
   All Craters within 40 yards of our line must be dealt with in this manner.
   The Commander on the spot is responsible for taking the necessary action.
   A Report will be rendered to Battn. H.Q. stating the action taken and a further report when the new trench has been completed and occupied.

(d) **BOMBARDMENT.** If during a Bombardment the men have to be withdrawn from the Front Line to dug-outs, "look-outs" under an Officer must be maintained in the Front line. Officers previously allotted must watch for the lift of the Artillery and at once occupy the Front line.
   Machine Guns and especially Lewis Guns and their teams will, when shell-proof cover exists, have their guns under cover during a bombardment. They must keep in touch with look-out men and be prepared to man their guns at the shortest notice. This does not apply to guns in permanent emplacements.

8. There is a wireless apparatus installed at Pt. G.4.9.3.3. which communicates direct with NOYELLES.

—— oOo ——

George M. Duncan. Lieut.
Adjutant 8th Seaforth Highlanders.

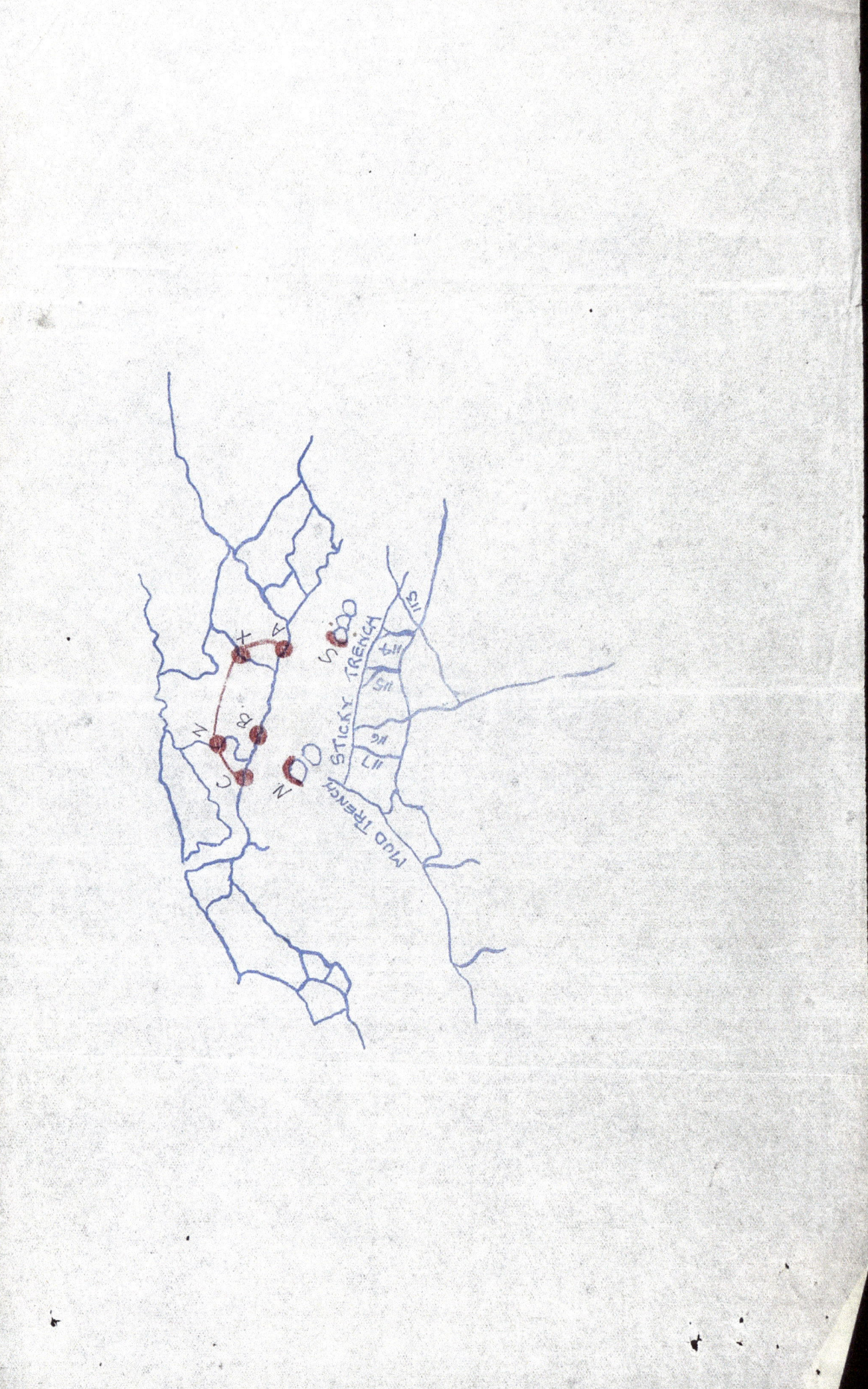

## APPENDIX
## "C" COMPANY.

No 10 Platoon. (Reserve)    Commander.- 2/Lieut. J. H Ross.
No. 3 Section.

| Duty. | Weapons. | Bombs. | S.A.A. | Tools. |
|---|---|---|---|---|
| =LEADER= | Rifle & Bayonet. | 3. | 120 rds. | |
| Bayonet Man. | Rifle & Bayonet. | 3. | 120 rds. | |
| Bomber. | Knob Kerrie. | 14. | | |
| Carrier. | | 23. | | 1 Bill Hook |
| Bayonet Man. | Rifle & Bayonet. | 3. | 120 rds. | |
| Bomber. | Knob Kerrie. | 14. | | |
| Carrier. | | 23. | | 1 Bill Hook |
| Looter. | Rifle & Bayonet. | 6. | 50 rds. | Knob Kerrie. |
| Bayonet Man. | Rifle & Bayonet. | 3. | 120 rds. | 1 Bill Hook |
| Bayonet Man. | Rifle & Bayonet. | 3. | 120 rds. | 1 Bill Hook |
| Spare Man. | Rifle & Bayonet. | 3. | 120 rds. | 1 Wire Cutters |
| Spare Man. | Rifle & Bayonet. | 3. | 120 rds | 1 Wire Cutters |
| | | 101. | 890 rds. | |

No. 4 Section.

| Duty. | Weapons. | Bombs. | S.A.A. | Tools. |
|---|---|---|---|---|
| =LEADER= | Rifle & Bayonet. | 3. | 120 rds. | |
| Bayonet Man. | Rifle & Bayonet. | 3. | 120 rds. | |
| Bomber. | Knob Kerrie. | 14. | | |
| Carrier. | | 23. | | 1 Bill Hook. |
| Bayonet Man. | Rifle & Bayonet. | 3. | 120 rds. | |
| Bomber. | Knob Kerrie. | 14. | | |
| Carrier. | | 23. | | 1 Bill Hook. |
| Looter. | Rifle & Bayonet. | 6. | 50 rds. | Knob Kerrie. |
| Bayonet Man. | Rifle & Bayonet. | 3. | 120 rds. | |
| Bayonet Man. | Rifle & Bayonet. | 3. | 120 rds. | |
| Spare Man. | Rifle & Bayonet. | 3. | 120 rds. | 1 pr Wire Cutters. |
| Spare Man. | Rifle & Bayonet. | 3. | 120 rds. | 1 pr Wire Cutters. |
| Spare Man. | Rifle & Bayonet. | 3. | 120 rds. | 1 Bill Hook. |
| Spare Man. | Rifle & Bayonet. | 3. | 120 rds. | 1 Bill Hook. |
| | | 107. | 1130 rds. | |

Note..- This was the Reserve Platoon in BOYAU 116.

APPENDIX      "C" Company.

No. 11 Platoon.                    Commander.- 2/Lieut. F.M McCallion.
No 1 Section.

| Duty. | Weapons. | Bombs. | S.A.A. | Tools. |
|---|---|---|---|---|
| =LEADER= | Knob Kerrie. | 6. | | |
| Bayonet Man. | Rifle & Bayonet. | 3. | 120 rds. | |
| Bomber. | | 12. | | 1 Bill Hook. |
| Carrier. | | 26. | | 1 Bill Hook. |
| Reserve Bomber. | | 12. | | 1 Bill Hook. |
| **No 2 Section.** | | | | |
| =LEADER= | Knob Kerrie. | 6. | | |
| Bayonet Man. | Rifle & Bayonet. | 3. | 120 rds. | |
| Bomber. | | 12. | | 1 Bill Hook. |
| Carrier. | | 26. | | 1 Bill Hook. |
| Bomber. | Knob Kerrie. | 12. | | |
| Carrier. | | 26. | | 1 Bill Hook. |
| **No 3 Section.** | | | | |
| =LEADER= | Knob Kerrie. | 6. | | |
| Bayonet Man. | Rifle & Bayonet. | 3. | 120 rds. | |
| Bomber. | | 12. | | 1 Bill Hook. |
| Carrier. | | 26. | | 1 Bill Hook. |
| Carrier. | | 26. | | 1 Bill Hook. |
| Bayonet Man. | Rifle & Bayonet. | 3. | 120 rds. | |
| **No 4 Section.** | | 12. | | 1 Bill Hook. |
| =LEADER= | | | | |
| Bayonet Man. | Rifle & Bayonet. | 3. | 120 rds. | |
| Bayonet Man. | Rifle & Bayonet. | 3. | 120 rds. | |
| Bomber. | Knob Kerrie. | 12. | | |
| Carrier. | Knob Kerrie. | 26. | | |
| Bomber. | | 12. | | 1 Bill Hook. |
| Carrier. | Knob Kerrie. | 26. | | |
| Bomber. | | 12. | | 1 Bill Hook. |
| Carrier. | | 26. | | 1 Bill Hook. |
| | | 352. | 720 rds. | |

NOTE. - 6 Wire Cutters and 6 Torch Lights distributed amongst Platoon.
The duty of this platoon was as follows:-
No 1 Section.   Establish block at Point "A".
No 2 Section.   Establish block on Communication Trench at Point "X".
No 3 Section.   To Stand at junction of Communication Trench and supply reliefs to either block.
No 4 Section.   To work up Fire Trench northwards, and meet "B" Coy.

## = APPENDIX IX.=
## "C" COMPANY

**No.13.Platoon.**      **Commander. 2/Lt.K.Mackenzie.**

No.1.Section.

| Duty. | Weapons. | Bombs. | S.A.A. | Tools. |
|---|---|---|---|---|
| =LEADER= | Rifle & Bayonet. | 3. | 120 rds. | 1 pr Wire Cutters. |
| Bayonet Man. | Rifle & Bayonet. | 3. | 120 rds. | 1 pr Wire Cutters & 1 Shovel. |
| Bomber. | Knob Kerrie. | 11. | - | - |
| Carrier. | Bayonet. | 23. | - | 1 Bill Hook. |
| Spare Man. | Rifle & Bayonet. | 3. | 120.rds | 1 Pick. |
| Bayonet Man. | Rifle & Bayonet. | 3. | 120.rds. | 1 pr Wire Cutters & 1 Shovel. |
| Bomber. | Knob Kerrie. | 11. | - | - |
| Carrier. | Bayonet. | 23. | - | 1 Bill Hook. |
| Bayonet Man. | Rifle & Bayonet. | 3. | 120.rds. | 1 pr Wire Cutters & 1 Shovel. |
| Bomber. | Knob Kerrie. | 11. | - | - |
| Carrier. | Bayonet. | 23. | - | 1 Bill Hook. |
| Spare Man. | Rifle & Bayonet. | 3. | 120.rds. | 1 Bill Hook & 1 Shovel. |
|  |  | 120. | 720.rds |  |

No.2.Section.

| Duty. | Weapon. | Bombs. | S.A.A. | Tools. |
|---|---|---|---|---|
| =LEADER= | Rifle & Bayonet. | 3. | 120.rds. | 1 pr Wire Cutters. |
| Bayonet Man. | Rifle & Bayonet. | 3. | 120.rds. | 1 pr Wire Cutters & 1 Shovel. |
| Bomber. | Knob Kerrie. | 11. | - | - |
| Carrier. | Bayonet. | 23. | - | 1 Bill Hook. |
| Spare Man. | Rifle & Bayonet. | 3. | 120.rds | 1.Shovel. |
| Bayonet Man. | Rifle & Bayonet. | 3. | 120.rds. | 1 pr Wire Cutters & 1 Shovel. |
| Bomber. | Knob Kerrie. | 11. | - | - |
| Carrier. | Bayonet. | 23. | - | 1 Bill Hook. |
| Bayonet Man. | Rifle & Bayonet. | 3. | 120.rds. | 1pr Wire Cutters & 1 Shovel. |
| Bomber. | Knob Kerrie. | 11. | - | - |
| Carrier. | Bayonet. | 23. | - | 1 Bill Hook. |
| Spare Man. | Rifle & Bayonet. | 3. | 120.rds. | 1 Bill Hook. |
|  |  | 120. | 720.rds. |  |

NOTE. The duty of this platoon was to seize & hold CRATER "S".
The platoon was accompanied by 1 Lewis Gun with team, each man of which was armed with 3 bombs and 8 drums of ammunition were carried for Lewis Gun.

SECRET

Operation Order
by
Lieut. Col. N. A. Thomson D.S.O.
Commdg 8th. Battn Seaforth Hghrs.

VII
No 3
Copy No 8

1. "A" and "C" Companies 8th Seaforth Hghrs will releive "A" and "B" Coys 7th Cameron Hghrs on July 11th in the left subsection HOHENZOLLERN SECTION.

2. Companies will releive in the following order:— "B" Coy 8th Seaforth Hghrs will releive "C" Coy 7th Cameron Hghrs in Right firing line.

"C" Coy 8th Seaforth Hghrs will releive "B" Coy 7th Cameron Hghrs in RESERVE TRENCH.— Guides (one per platoon) from "A" Coy 7th Cameron Hghrs will meet "B" Coy 8th Seaforth Hghrs at junction of QUARRY ALLEY and CANNON STREET at 9 a.m. 11th July.

Guides (one per platoon) from "B" Coy 7th Cameron Hghrs will meet "C" Coy 8th Seaforth Hghrs, at junction of QUARRY ALLEY and CANNON STREET at 9-15 a.m. 11th July.

Route for "B" Coy 8th Seaforths :— QUARRY ALLEY, GUILDFORD TRENCH, NORTHAMPTON TRENCH.

Route for "C" Coy. QUARRY ALLEY

3. Advanced parties to take over trench stores will be at Headqrs "A" and "B" Coy. 7th Cameron Hghrs at 6-30 a.m. 11th inst.— Receipts to be rendered to Battn Headquarters by 6 p.m. 11th inst.

4. Guides (one per gun) for Lewis Guns will be at junction of QUARRY ALLEY and CANNON STREET at 9-45 a.m.— Lewis Gun Officer 8th Seaforth Hghrs will supply guides (one per gun) for guns of 7th Cameron Hghrs under arrangements to be made by him with Lewis Gun Officer, 7th Cameron

5. One guide from Snipers 7th Cameron Hghrs will be at junction of QUARRY ALLEY and CANNON STREET at 8-30 a.m to guide Snipers 8th Seaforth Hghrs to their position in the line.

6. Headquarters personnel 8th Seaforth Hghrs at present in LANCASHIRE TRENCH will releive Headqrs 7th Cameron Hghrs at junction of QUARRY ALLEY and CANNON STREET at 10. a.m.

7. Completion of relief to be reported to Battn Headquarters by wire.

Donald MacLachlan
Lieutenant.
Adjutant. 8th Battn Seaforth Hghrs.

Copy No 1.— O.C. 7th Cameron Hrs.   No 5.— O.C. "D" Coy. for information.
    2.— O.C. "B" Coy.              6.— Lewis Gun Officer.
    3.— O.C. "C" Coy.              7.— Sniping Officer.
    4.— OC "A" Coy. for information. 8.— File.

## APPENDIX.

## "C" COMPANY.

**No.9. Platoon.**  Commander. 2/Lt.C.Forrest.

### No.1.Section.

| Duty. | Weapon. | Bombs. | S.A.A. | Tools. |
|---|---|---|---|---|
| =LEADER= | Rifle & Baynet. | 3. | 120. rds. | 1.pr Wire Cutters. |
| Bayonet Man. | Rifle & Bayonet. | 3. | 120. rds. | 1.pr Wire Cutters. |
| Bomber. | Knob Kerry. | 11. | — | 1 Shovel. |
| Carrier. | | 23. | — | 1.Bill Hook. |
| Bomber. | Knob Kerry. | 11. | — | 1.Pick. |
| Carrier. | | 23. | — | 1.Bill Hook. |
| Bayonet Man. | Rifle & Bayonet. | 3. & 1 Smoke Bomb. | 120. rds. | 1.pr Wire Cutters & 1.Ladder. |
| Bayonet Man. | Rifle & Bayonet. | 3 & 2 Smoke Bombs. | 120. rds. | 1.pr Wire Cutters & 1 Ladder. |
| Looter. | | 6. | — | 1.Bill Hook. 1.Ladder. 1.Loot Bag. |
| Spare Man. | Rifle & Bayonet. | 3. | 60. rds | 1.Ladder. |
| Platoon Sergt. | Rifle & Bayonet. | 3. | 120. rds | 1.Grappling Iron. |
| | | 97. | 660. | |

### No.2.Section.

| Duty. | Weapon. | Bombs. | S.A.A. | Tools. |
|---|---|---|---|---|
| =LEADER= | Rifle & Bayonet. | 3. | 120 rds. | 1 pr Wire Cutters. |
| Bayonet Man. | Rifle and Bayonet. | 3. | 120 rds. | 1 pr Shear wire Cutters. |
| Bomber. | Knob Kerrie. | 11. | — | 1 Pick. |
| Carrier. | Knob Kerrie. | 23. | — | 1pr Wire Cutters. |
| Bayonet Man. | Rifle & Bayonet. | 3. | 120 rds. | 1 pr Wire Cutters & 1 Bill Hook. |
| Bayonet Man. | Rifle & Bayonet. | 3. | 120 rds. | 1 pr Wire Cutters & 1 Shovel. |
| Bayonet Man. | Rifle & Bayonet. | 3. | 120 rds. | 1 pr Wire Cutters & 1 Shovel. |
| Bayonet Man. | Rifle & Bayonet. | 3. | 120 rds. | 1 pr Wire Cutters & 1 Pick. |
| Bayonet Man. | Rifle & Bayonet. | 3 & 2 Smoke Bombs. | 120 rds. | 1 Bill Hook. |
| | Rifle & Bayonet. | 3. | 120 rds. | 1 Bill Hook. 1 Shovel. 1.Loot Bag. |
| Bayonet Man. | Rifle & Bayonet. | 3 & 2 Smoke Bombs. | 120 rds. | 1 Pick. 1 Bill Hook. |
| Bayonet Man. | Rifle & Bayonet. | 3. | 120 rds. | 1 Bill Hook. |
| | | 64. | 1200 rds. | |

NOTE. The duty of this platoon was as follows:-
No.1 Sedtion. To support the Raiding party of No 11 Platoon, bombing all dug-outs etc.
No 2 Section. To provide sentries on the enemy's parados & to beat of enemy if he counter-attacks across the open from his Support Line.

Report on state of Enemy trenches from
Information gathered during raid on 10/11th July 1916.

**I. FIRE TRENCH.** The general lines are the same as our own. The trench is broken up into Bays by strong traverses. The line is irregular according to the nature of the ground. Depth about 10ft 6ins

**COMMUNICATION TRENCH.** Very deep, about 11ft. In other respects much the same as our own.

**II. REVETTMENTS.** The trenches are well revetted throughout. A certain number of sandbags have been used but the material generally in use is wood bound together with fencing wire.

**III. FIRE-STEPS.** The fire steps are about 5ft 6ins from the bottom of the trench. There are 3 steps up. The 1st step is cut out of the earth & is revetted. Height about 3ft. The two top steps are built of wood. Height about 15". Breadth about 18 inches to 2 feet.

**IV. DUG-OUTS.** Dugouts are numerous & entrances are all on the firestep side of the trench. From the outside they appear to be very much the same as our deep dugouts. Some dugouts are fitted with wooden doors. One dugout was noticed with an entrance on the side of a traverse; this entrance was fitted with a wooden door.

**V. CONDITION OF TRENCHES.** The condition of the trenches was good. In places they had been blown in by our artillery. They appear to be maintained by skilled pioneers.
The trenches are fitted with duckboards of much the same pattern as those used by us. Some parts were reported to be without duckouts; possibly they were unnoticed being covered with earth.

## Appendix.
## "B" Company.

### No 8 platoon.   Commander Lieut T.C. GRANT.

**No 1 & 2 Sections** (12 men in each).

1. Leader.
2. Bayonet Man.
3. Bayonet Man.
4. "      "    Carrying pick
5. "      "      "    shovel.
6. "      "      "    pick.
7. "      "      "    shovel.
8. "      "      "    pick.
9. "      "      "    shovel.
10. "     "      "    pick.
11. "     "      "    shovel.
12. Bomb carrier with 2 buckets each containing 12 bombs.

Each man of this platoon carries 4 bombs each & 120 rounds S.A.A.
The duty of this platoon was to seize & hold Crater "N".
1 Lewis Gun & team was attached to No 8 platoon.

### No 6 platoon.

**No 3 & 4 Sections** (12 men in each).   Commander Lieut A.J.M. MILLER

1. Leader.
2. Bomber with bill hook.
3.  "     "   "    "
4. Bayonet Man.
5. Bomber with Knob Kerrie.
6.  "     "    "    "
7. Bayonet Man.
8. Bomber with Knob Kerrie.
9.  "     "    "    "
10. Bayonet Man.
11. Bayonet Man.
12. Bomber with Knob Kerrie.

Carriers — 2 men each carrying 2 buckets of bombs, 1 man carrying tape
Bombers — Each bomber carries 6 bombs in pouches & 12 in a satchel.
Bayonet Man — Each carried 6 bombs & 50 rounds S.A.A.
The duty of this platoon was to rush point B & establish blocks at pts "C" & "Z".

## Appendix.

## "B" Company

No 7 Platoon.                                    Commander Lieut J.E. SMITH.

No 5 & 6 Sections (12 men in each).

1. Leader.
2. Bomber with Knobkerrie.
3. Bayonet Man.
4. Bomber with Knobkerrie.
5. Bayonet Man.
6. Carries pick.
7. Bomber with bill hook.
8. Bayonet Man.
9. Bomber with Knobkerrie.
10. Carries pick.
11. Looter carrying tape.
12. Looter     "     Knobkerrie & "P" bomb.

Carriers — 1 N.C.O. & 5 men carrying 1 bucket of bombs each.
Bombers — Each bomber carries 6 bombs in his pouches & 12 in a satchel.
Bayonet Man — Each man carries 6 Bombs & 50 rounds S.A.A.
This platoon follows No 6 platoon.

No 5 Platoon.                                    Commander Lieut J.J. WILSON

No 7 & 8 Sections.

No 7
1. Leader.
2. Bomber with bill hook
3. Bayonet Man.
4.    "        "
5. Bomber with Knobkerrie.
6. Bayonet Man.
7. Bayonet Man.
8. Bomber with bill hook.
9. Looter with Knob kerrie.
10. Looter with Knob kerrie.
11. Spareman carrying 2 Buckets Bombs.

No 8
1. Leader.
2. Bomber with knobkerrie
3.    "        "      "
4. Bayonet Man.
5. Bomber with Knob kerrie.
6. Bomber with Bill hook.
7. Bayonet Man.
8. Looter with Knob kerrie.
9. Spareman carrying "P" bomb.

Bombers. Each bomber carries 6 Bombs in pouches & 12 in a satchel
Bayonet Men    "    man carries 6 Bombs in pouches & 50 rounds S.A.A.
This platoon followed No 7 platoon.

O.C. all Companies.                                8th. Battalion Seaforth Highlanders
                                                                D. 65.

Following Mining Working Parties required while Battalion is in Brigade Support:-

"A" Company.   1 N.C.O. & 20 men for 180th.(T) Coy. R.E. to rendezvous at
               Junction of FOSSE WAY and O.B.1. 9.10 a.m., at 3.30 p.m.,
               at 9.30 p.m. and at 3.30. a.m.

"B" Company.   1 N.C.O. and 15 men form 170th.(T) Coy. R.E., to rendezvous
               at junction of BARTS ALLEY and NORTHAMPTON TRENCH at 8.a.m.

"C" Company.   1 N.C.O. and 15 men for 170th. (T) Coy. R.E. to rendezvous
               at junction of BARTS ALLEY and NORTHAMPTON TRENCH at 4 p.m.

"D" Company.   1 N.C.O. and 15 men for 170th. (T) Coy. R.E. to rendezvous
               at junction of BARTS ALLEY and NORTHAMPTON TRENCH at 12m.n.

               1 N.C.O. and 25 men for 180th.(T) Coy. R.E. to rendezvous
               at Junction of FOSSE WAY and O.B.6., at 5.p.m. and 11 p.m.

These Parties will commence for 170th. Coy. R.E. at 4 p.m. and for 180th.
Coy. at 8.p.m.


                                                                    Lieut.,
July 5th. 1916.    Adjutant 8th. Battalion Seaforth Highlanders.

SECRET — 8th SEAFORTH HIGHLANDERS —
DEFENCE SCHEME   **III**
← BRIGADE SUPPORT - HOHENZOLLERN SECTION →

[1.] The Section extends from BOYAU 94 (G.11.b.8½.2) CAMPBELL'S CUT (exclusive) to MUD ALLEY (G.4.a.8.8) inclusive and is divided into 3 Sub-Sections.
RIGHT-SUB-SECTION — From right of Section to BOYAU 101 (inclusive)
CENTRE SUB-SECTION — From BOYAU 101 (exclusive) to BOYAU 109 (inclusive)
LEFT-SUB-SECTION — From BOYAU 109 (exclusive) to Left of Section.

[2.] GARRISON:— 1 Battalion occupies each Sub-section.
1 Battalion in Brigade Support occupies RAILWAY RESERVE TRENCH including JUNCTION and CENTRAL KEEPS, and LANCASHIRE TRENCH.   HEADQUARTERS:— CANNON STREET.

[3.] COMMUNICATIONS:—
Rt. Sub-Section { "UP" — HULLUCH ALLEY - O.B.4 - FOSSE WAY.
                 DOWN — STANSFIELD ROAD - HULLUCH ALLEY. }
CENTRE Sub-Section { "UP" — HULLUCH ALLEY.
                     "DOWN" — GORDON ALLEY. }
LEFT Sub-Section { "UP" — QUARRY ALLEY.
                   "DOWN" — BARTS ALLEY. }

NOTE: FOSSE WAY is inclusive to the HULLUCH SECTION but is used to both Sections. O.C. Coys. will post Controls on Communication Trenches in their Coy. areas to regulate Traffic. Sentries will be provided with written orders that no-one except (a) Staff Officers including Battn. Staff (b) Signal Runners & Linesmen (c) Officers with a pass signed by Brigade Major, may use UP and DOWN Trenches in an unauthorized direction.

[4] ACTION IN CASE OF ATTACK:—
(a) Artillery Support will be called for by 'S.O.S' Signal on the Telephone or by firing Green Rockets in quick succession from Company or Battalion Headquarters when communication by Telephone has failed. At least 12 of these rockets with apparatus for firing them, will be kept at all Coy. and Battalion H.Q.'s in the Trenches. These signals and Rockets are only to be used when in the opinion of the Officer on the Spot the immediate establishment of an Artillery Barrage is necessary and an Infantry attack is advancing.
(b) O.C. Coys. will make themselves and their Officers thoroughly acquainted with the general Trench System, and thoroughly reconnoitre the portions in which they may be called upon to act.
(c) Battn. will stand to arms.
(d) Working parties in Trenches east of and including VILLAGE LINE will report to nearest Battalion Commander, and O.C. Battn. concerned, will use them as he thinks fit.
(e) ARRANGEMENTS for BOMB CARRYING.
O.C "A" Coy. will detail 3 platoons to carry from RESERVE STORE in CLARKE'S KEEP to Brigade Advanced Store as under:—
(1) at junction of O.B.2 & FOSSE WAY.
(2) at junction of GORDON ALLEY and CLIFFORD STREET.
(3) In CANNON STREET off QUARRY ALLEY — etc
One Platoon serving each.

O.C. "B" Coy. will detail:—
1 Platoon to carry from Brigade Advanced Store at Junction of O.B.2 & FOSSE WAY to Right Battn. Grenade Store in O.G.2 between GOEBEN ALLEY and FOSSE WAY.

½ Platoon to carry from Brigade Advanced Store at Junction of GORDON ALLEY and CLIFFORD STREET to the Centre Battn. Grenade Store at junction of GORDON ALLEY and O.B.1
(Cont'd)

(2).

(cont'd)

½ Platoon to carry from Brigade Advanced Store in CANNON STREET to the Left. Battn. Store in the QUARRY.

NOTE:- All these platoons and half-platoons must contain 30 and 15 men respectively. They must at once reconnoitre the Trenches and learn the way to stores to which they have to carry.

Should any men told off to carry bombs be working, they will at once be marched to their bomb store as warned.

[5]. SPECIAL INSTRUCTIONS:-

(a) GAS:- The code signals to denote attack by gas is "S.O.S -GAS-" followed by Company reporting. Troops will at once put on their Gas Helmets and be kept as still as possible; no movement must be allowed except that necessary to man the Trenches. A STROMBUS HORN will be sounded at Brigade and each Battn. Headquarters directly a GAS message is received. As soon as the cloud has passed O.C Coys. will report at once to Battn. H.Q. the condition of the men stating to what extent they have been affected by the gas.

GAS Helmets are not to be removed until ordered from Battn. H.Q.

In the event of a gas attack it is most important that messages be passed from front to rear.

———~———ooo———~———

George W. Duncan.

Lieut.,
Adjutant, 8th Battn. Seaforth Highlanders.,

July. 5th 1916.

SECRET.   Operation Order No 2.   Copy No. 4
by
Lieut Col. N.A. Thomson D.S.O.   **IV**
Cmdg 8 Seaforth Highlanders.

10th July 1916.

1. "A" & "D" Coys 8th Seaforth Hdrs. will relieve "C" & "D" Companies 7th Cameron Hdrs on 10th July 1916 in the left subsection HOHENZOLLERN SECTION.

2. Companies will relieve in following order.
   "D" Coy 8th S.H. will relieve "C" Coy 7th C.H. in CENTRE FIRING LINE
   "A" Coy  "   "   "   "   "D" Coy  "   "   LEFT   "   "
   Guides (one per platoon) from "C" Coy 7th C.H. will meet "D" Coy 8th S.H. at junction of Quarry Alley & Railway Reserve Trench at 9 A.M. 10th July.
   Guides (one per platoon) from "D" Coy 7th C.H. will meet "A" Coy 8th S.H. at junction of Quarry Alley & Cannon Street at 9.15 A.M. 10th July.
   Route for "D" Coy - QUARRY ALLEY.
   "   "   "A" Coy  "   "   DEVIATION, MUD ALLEY.

3. Platoons at present garrisoning JUNCTION KEEP & CENTRAL KEEP will be relieved by platoons of 7th C.H. at 7.30 A.M. 10th July. Guides (1 per keep) will be sent to meet platoons of 7th C.H. at junction of RESERVE TRENCH & QUARRY ALLEY at 7 A.M. 10th July.

4. Advanced parties to take over trench stores will be at HQrs "C" & "D" Coys 7th C.H. at 6.30 A.M. 10th inst. Receipts to be rendered to Battn HQrs by 6 pm 10th inst.

5. All Lewis Guns will remain in present positions.

6. Completion of relief to be reported to Battn HQrs.

Copy No 1 OC A Coy    No 3. M.G.O.       George W Duncan
     2. OC D Coy     No 4. FILE                Lt & Adjt
     3 OC B Coy  } For Information        8 Seaforth Hdrs
     6 OC C Coy  }

SECRET.   **V**   D 115.

1. With reference to para 7 of 8th Seaforth Highlanders Operation Order No 1 dated 10th July 1916.

   (a) The password will be "DINGWALL."

   (b) Hour of Zero will be 11.30 p.m.

2. Acknowledge.

George W. Duncan
Lt & Adj,
8/Seaforth Highlanders

Issued at 12.30 pm
Through Signals
To all recipients of the above-mentioned order.

10/7/16.

Report on Operations in LEFT SUB-SECTION.
HOHENZOLLERN SECTION.
10/11th July, 1916.

1. The Operations were successfully carried out by Captain's Holmes & Hart, Commanding "B" & "C" Company respectively, under Major G.M. Lumsden.

2. The starting point was left punctually at the hour fixed and watches were synchronised at Battalion Headquarters.

3. Companies were in position as under at 10-30.P.M. "B" Company in STICKY TRENCH facing North with its head at Sap 13 (Pt G.4.b.2.7.), followed by detachment of 74th Field Company, R.E.

"C" Company; No's 11 & 12 platoons in Mine Shafts near BOYAU 115, & No.10 & 9 platoons in NORTHAMPTON TRENCH North of BOYAU 116.

4. A gap having been prepared in the Eastern side of Sap 13, "B" Company commenced to file through it at 11-5.P.M.

5. At 11-30.P.M. the Mine was exploded near RUSSIAN SAP. At this moment, "B" Company had 3 complete platoons through our wire and lying immediately South of Crater N, facing the enemy and the 4th platoon, just clear of the Sap. A good deal of debris from the Mine, fell in the neighbourhood of this Company and one man had his leg broken. Although prepared for the Mine explosion, reports agree the shock was considerable. This shews that in the enemy's lines & Saps near Crater S, the effect must have been very great.

6. Immediately the Mine debris had fallen the Crater N was occupied by No.8 platoon under 2/Lt.J.C.Grant and fire was opened on the enemy's trenches to the North East. Crater N were unoccupied by the enemy which confirm reports from previous patrols. The remainder rushed the enemy's lines at & near point B; Captain Holmes with a portion of it, bombed his way towards point A engaging the enemy who at some points threw bombs from behind their parados. Entrance to the enemy's trenches were effected by No.6. platoon North of point B. A Block was formed at point Z and a party of this platoon worked a considerable way Northwards beyond point C where a Block was to have been established. N.CO's who were this party, report the enemy were shelling their own front line and that the trenches were full of dead and wounded Germans. Captain Holmes got into personal touch with Captain Hart, Commanding C Company on Crater S.
"C" Company left NORTHAMPTON TRENCH and the two Mine Shafts near BOYAU 115 immediately the debris from our Mine had fallen.
1 platoon under 2/Lt F.McCallion rushed the enemy trenches at point A. 1 platoon with Lewis Gun seized Crater S and opened fire to the South & South East. No.9. platoon followed 2/Lt McCallion's platoon into the enemy trenches at point A while the 4th platoon moved up. BOYAU 116 to Major Lumsden's Headquarters as arranged.
2/Lt McCallion's platoon established Blocks and worked Northwards along enemy's fire trench.
Between points A & B a machine gun which could not be removed, was smashed up and bombed. About 12 dugouts and Mine Shafts were bombed, a few who came out of them, were bayonet and shot; some of the dugouts had lights in them. Groans and other noises were heard after the bombing.
A young Cadet Officer of the 23rd Bavarian Regiment was captured and brought over to our lines; he was unarmed having left his revolver in his dugout.

# SECRET.

4 Continued:-

(c) An Advanced Report Centre has been prepared in the Fire Trench, immediately North of its junction with BOYAU 16, from which communications by telephone is established to Battalion Headquarters and also to Artillery (latter arranged by O.C.71st Battery,R.F.A.) and to 170th Tunnelling Company,R.E., by an Electric Bell.

5.

(a) ACTION minus 30 minutes.
"D" Company, followed by R.E., will commence to file out of Sap 12 as explained personally to O.C."D"Company and should be in position outside our wire by minus 10 minutes.

(b) ACTION at minus 5 minutes.
"B" Company, followed by R.E., will commence to crawl towards point B.

(c) ACTION AT ZERO HOUR.
Under direction of O.C."B"Company,- platoon together with Lewis Gun will seize Crater N.
The remaining 3 platoons of "B"Company, followed by R.E., will rush GERMAN TRENCHES at point B.
The MINE referred to in para r(d) will be exploded by 170th Company,R.E. (The near lip of the Crater formed by this mine will be consolidated by a party of "D"Company 8th Battn.Seaforth Highdrs, under arrangements which are being made by O.C.Left Sub-Section(Lieut.Colonel. C.H.Haigh.,D.S.O., 7th Battn Cameron Highdrs)
From ZERO HOUR onwards for 40 minutes, certain guns and Trench Mortars will bombard the enemy's front line from point G.4.b.4.9 northwards and back of Craters from point G.4.b.4.1.southwards;on latter area,rifle grenades, and Mills Bombs from cup attachment will be freely used.
From ZERO HOUR,our guns will also barrage HINDENBURG TRENCH, the enemy's Support Trench between HINDENBURG & CROSS TRENCH,and CROSS TRENCH east of the enemy's Support line,for 40 minutes(i.e.until 40 minutes after the withdrawal hour)

5. (d) ACTION 1 Minute after ZERO HOUR.
Under direction of O.C."C" Company,- platoon together with Lewis Gun will seize Crater S.
3 platoons will rush GERMAN TRENCHES at point A.
1 platoon will move up BOYAU A 6 to its junction with STICKYE TRENCH and report at Advanced Report Centre for orders.

6. WITHDRAWAL.

(a) No order will be given to "retire". All men must be warned against enemy ruses. Anyone using this word will be shot.

(b) At,0.40.minutes, buglers from our front trench will sound "ORDERLY SERGEANTS" to call attention to this hour having been reached.

(c) The platoons of "B" & "C" Companies holding the Craters (N & S) will remain till the last and cover the retirement of their respective Companies.

(d) Blocking Parties will remain at their posts until our raiding parties are clear of the enemy's trench.

(e) "P" Bombs will be dropped to cover the retirement.

(f) Companies will normally retire by the point at which they entered but the alternative routes, via point A or B. should be borne in mind.

SECRET.                                                        Copy.No. 13

Operation Order No.1.
by
Lieut;Colonel.N.A.Thomson,D.S.O. 10ᵃ
Comdg;8th(Service)Battalion.Seaforth Highlanders, 7th July,1916.

Reference attached sketch,and trench map.1/10,000.

"B"&"C" Companies 8th(Service)Battalion.Seaforth Highlanders
with a detachment of 1 Officer,2 N.C.O's & 6 men Royal Engineers
under Major.G.M.Lumsden will raid the enemy's trenches on the
night of 10/11th July,1916,under the following plan:-

1.      OBJECT of RAID.
          To kill all Germans,cut all telephone wires,bomb all dugouts,
destroy or capture all Machine Guns & Trench Mortars & damage
all Mine Shafts within the area C.Z.,and to return to our trenches
on completion with prisoners and other identifications.
*The raid is intended to take the form of a Surprise.*

2.      LIMITS of RAID.
          Enemy's front line and communication trenches as defined
above only.  There is to be no pressing on to the support line or
beyond the blocks which will be formed at C.Z.X.A.,at about 50
yards each from the points of junction of front line with
communication trenches,as shewn on sketch.

3.      DURATION of RAID.
          30 minutes from Zero.

4. (a)  PREPARATIONS for the ASSAULT.
          Enemy wire has been cut at various points in the line
including points A & B.
   (b)    Companies will march to rendez-vous as under:-

STARTING POINT.   Junction of QUARRY ALLEY & LANCASTER TRENCH.
TIME.             Minus 2½ hours.
ORDER of MARCH.   "B"Company,followed by 1 Lewis Gun & Team,and
                  1 Officer,2 N.C.O's & 6 men R.E.
                  ROUTE. QUARRY ALLEY,BOYAU 116,STICKY TRENCH to
                            Sap 13(pt G.4.D.4.7.)
                  "C"Company,followed by 1 Lewis Gun & Team.
                  ROUTE. QUARRY ALLEY,NORTHAMPTON TRENCH.

          11 & 12 platoons "C"Company & 1 Lewis Gun will proceed to
Mine Shafts already alloted.
          9 & 10 platoons "C"Company will remain in NORTHAMPTON TRENCH.
   (c)  Gaps in our wire have been made between BOYAU 116 & Sap 13;at each
of these gaps,ladders will be placed by O.C."B"Company by 7.P.M.
10th July,1916.
          Similar gaps have been made between BOYAU 116 & BOYAU 111;ladders
will be placed at each of these gaps by O.C."C"Company by 7.P.M.,
10th July,1916. *for use in the case of necessity.*
   (d)  O.C.170th Tunnelling Company has prepared a Mine at a point about
60 yards N.E.from N.E.end of RUSSIAN SAP

6. Continued:-

(g) On return to oure trenches, all men will go direct to LANCASHIRE TRENCH as under:-
"B" Company, via MUD ALLEY, DEVIATION TRENCH & QUARRY ALLEY.
"C" Company, via BARTS ALLEY.
It has been arranged by O.C. Left Sub-Section that Controls will be posted as under:-
1 Officer & 1 N.C.O. at the junction of the RESERVE TRENCH and QUARRY ALLEY.
1 N.C.O. at the junction of the RESERVE TRENCH & LEFT BOYAU.
1 Officer & 1 N.C.O. at the junction of RESERVE TRENCH and BARTS ALLEY.
These Control Posts will take the names & regimental numbers of all men returning to LANCASHIRE TRENCH.

7. MEDICAL arrangements.
All wounded will be brought back either by QUARRY ALLEY or BARTS ALLEY.
Dressing Stations are as follows:-
  1. At the S.E. corner of the QUARRY, recently used as a Bomb Store.
  2. In BARTS ALLEY, near its junction with RESERVE TRENCH.
  3. In QUARRY ALLEY near its junction with CANNON STREET.

8. PRISONERS.
Any prisoners who may be captured are to be sent without delay to Battalion Headquarters and there handed over to the Provost Sergeant. A receipt will be taken.

9. T I M E.
All watches will be synchronised at Headquarters, 8th Battn. Seaforth Highdrs, 2 hours before ZERO hour.

10. REPORTS.
All reports afetr minus 1½ hours to Advance Report Centre mentioned in par. 4(e).

11. MISCELLANEOUS.
No letters or papers, badges or numerals will be carried on the personnal taking part in the raid.
Identity Disc will be worn.
ZERO HOUR and PASSWORD will be notified later.

12. SPECIAL PRECAUTIONS.
In case the officer Commanding the raiding party (Major G.M.Lumsden) should consider it adviseable after minus 30 minutes to hasten the ZERO HOUR, the following arrangements have been made:-
(1) The electric Bell will be rung to warn 170th Tunnelling Company, R.E., to explode the mine.
(2) The Artillery Liaison officer will warn the Artillery to at once open fire in accordance with programme normally timed for ZERO HOUR.
(3) "B" & "C" Companies will act according to arrangements made for the normal hour ZERO HOUR.

................George W Duncan........ Lieutenant.
8th(Ser)Battalion, Seaforth Highlanders.

Distribution
Copy No 1. Major G.M.Lumsden) 8th Sea Highrs
No 2. O.C. B. Coy.
No 3. O.C. C. Coy.
No 4. O.C. 7th Cameron Highrs
No 5 - 12 Headquarters 44th Inf Bde.
No 13. War Diary
No 14. File.

Continued:-

7. The raiding parties withdrew at 12 midnight, at which hour a Bugler sounded "Orderly Sergeants" from our front line. Some small parties of "C" Company remained a few minutes after this hour, not having heard the call and being unaware of the time.

8. Crater N was shelled by the enemy about half way through the operation and during the latter part of it, the enemy shelled his own front line. A machine gun from AD point played on "B" Company early in the operations but was not very effective.

9. The enemy wire was very well cut near both points near A & B. This confirms reports from patrols previously carried out by Lieutenant J.E. Smith.

10. Our Artillery barrage appears to have been very effective and gave our men great confidence.

11. Unfortunately 2/Lieutenant WARE, Royal Engineers was killed on the German parapet and four of his men were wounded about the same time. Both he and his small detachment behaved in great gallantry.

12. (a) There was a threequarter moon which did not appear very favourable to our operation but possibly this prevented a greater use by the enemy of VERY LIGHTS which was normal.
    (b) Long grass favoured the raid.
    (c) 1 Company blackened their faces and hands with burnt cork, this prevented them shewing up so much at night and helped Officers to recognise their own men.
    (d) Knob Kerries and Bill Hooks were found useful; bayonets were not fixed till in the enemy trenches.
    (e) "C" Company's Lewis Gun jammed after firing two drums.
    (f) Reports of our recent successes on the SOMME were left in trenches as a souvenir.

13. It is estimated that the German losses exclusive of those from our Artillery fire were at least one hundred men.
    Our casualties were as follows:-
    Killed....1 Officer, R.E.
              6 O.R. Seaforth Highdrs.
    Wounded...6 Officers & 57 O.R.

14. Much material was destroyed in enemy trenches, and the following articles were brought back to our lines:-
    5 German Rifles.
    3 Gas Masks.
    1 Searchlight.
    1 Bayonet.

15. The names of Officers & O.R., who did specially good work in this raid will be forwarded under separate cover.

16. The appendix are attached.
    Sketch Map.
    Information as to nature, construction and condition of enemy trenches.
    Orginization of platoons which took part in the raid.

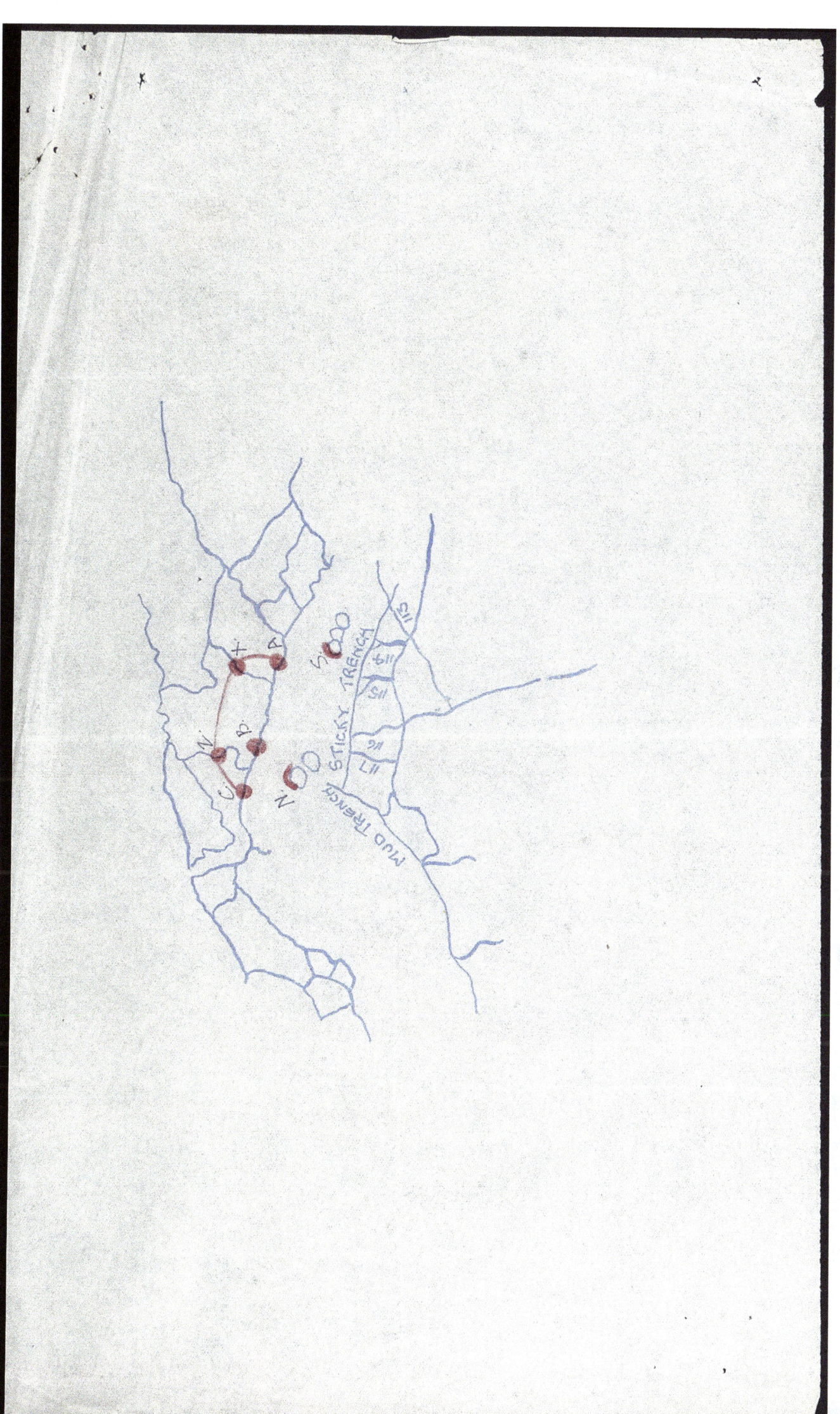

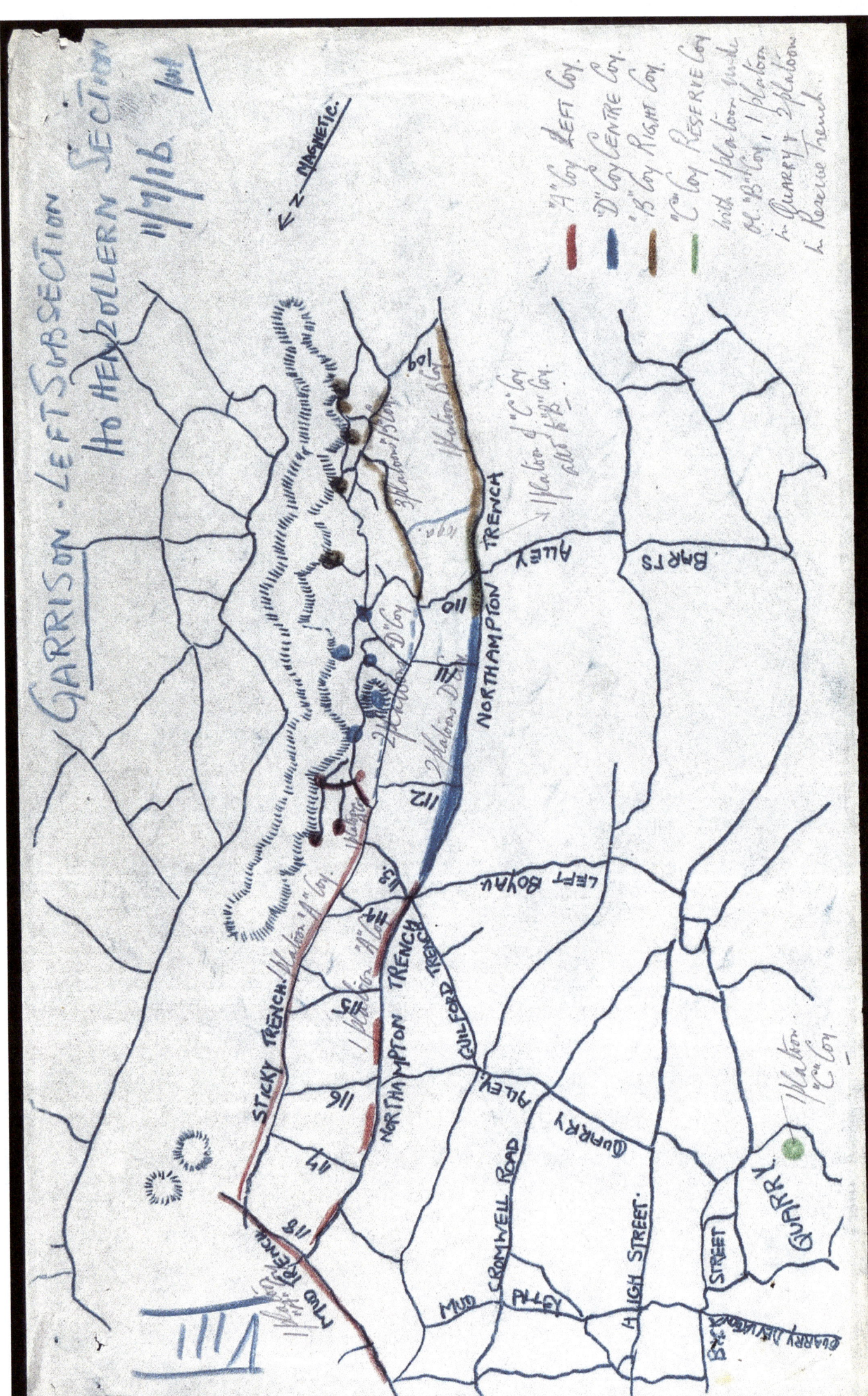

## Appendix

### Bomb Posts and Grenade Stores

1. The front line will be held by Bombing Posts in the HAIRPIN and HOHENZOLLERN SECTORS. Each of these are to contain 4 boxes of bombs at the Bombing post, and a Grenade Store containing 12 boxes and 48 Mills Bombs and 16 Grenade Haversacks at the base of each sap where it joins the firing line.

2. SUPPORT LINE – In addition to the Garrison of the Support line the Support line will be held by Bombing posts. These are situated in the Support line at its junction with all communication trenches running to the front line.

   There are stores at these points as under:-

   | | TOTAL GRENADES |
   |---|---|
   | Junction of NORTHAMPTON TRENCH with BARTS ALLEY | 480 |
   | "    "    "    "    "    "    CORK STREET | 480 |
   | "    "    "    "    "    "    GUILDFORD TR. | 480 |
   | "    "    "    "    "    "    QUARRY ALLEY | 180 |

3. RESERVE LINE

   | | |
   |---|---|
   | Junction with BARTS ALLEY | 3,600 |
   | "    "    LEFT BOYAU | 180 |
   | "    "    QUARRY ALLEY | 180 |
   | IN THE QUARRY | 3,600 |

   BRIGADE ADVANCED STORE

   | | |
   |---|---|
   | Junction of O.B.2 with FOSSE WAY | 6000 |
   | "    "    GORDON ALLEY with CLIFFORD STREET | 7,200 |
   | IN CANNON STREET off QUARRY ALLEY | 7,200 |

   BRIGADE RESERVE STORE.

   | | |
   |---|---|
   | CLARKES KEEP, VERMELLES | 14,400 |

4. O.C. Support Battn. will nominate parties from LANCASHIRE TRENCH to carry Grenades forward at once as under
   (1) 1 Platoon to carry from Brigade Advanced store at junction of O.B.2 and FOSSE WAY to Rr. Battn. Grenade store in O.G.R. between GOEBEN ALLEY and FOSSE WAY.

SECRET.
— 8th Seaforth Highlanders —
P.147

O.C. "B" Coy.
O.C. "C" Coy.
O.C. "A" Coy.  ⎫
O.C. "D" Coy.  ⎬ For Information.
M.G.O          ⎭

(1) "C" Coy. will relieve "B" Coy. in the Right Firing Line to-morrow, 16th July, 1916, under arrangements to be made between O.s.C. Companies concerned.

(2) I Platoon of "B" Coy. will remain in the line & on the relief being completed will come under the orders of O.C. "C" Coy.

(3) Bombers will be relieved first — the whole relief should be complete by 9. a.m.

(4) Acknowledge.

———~———

July 15th 1916.

George W. Duncan
Lieut,
Adjutant, 8th Seaforth His.

To The Adjutant.  
Seaforth Highrs.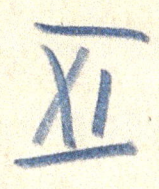

It seems possible that the enemy opposite us has been relieved today as they are of what one might call of a "friendly nature". They are exposing themselves very much and are throwing pieces of chalk into our saps heads and are waving to our men with their caps. Their caps are of grey material with a small button in front and grey tunics. Probably greenish gray would be near the colour.

I have warned all ranks to be very careful tonight.

Murray Capt  
C. Company  
17-7-16

Time 9-40 pm

"C" Form (Duplicate).  
MESSAGES AND SIGNALS.

Army Form C. 2123.
(In books of 50's in duplicate.)
No. of Message ..................

| | Charges to Pay. | Office Stamp. |
| --- | --- | --- |
| | £ s. d. | |
| Service Instructions. | | |

Handed in at .................... Office ........... m. Received ........... m.

TO

| Sender's Number | Day of Month | In reply to Number | AAA |
| --- | --- | --- | --- |
| | | | |

FROM  
PLACE & TIME

Wt. 432—M497 500,000 Pads. H W V 5/16 Forms C.2123.

Intelligence Report:
to noon 19/7/16. **XII**

1. At 2.30pm. yesterday a party of 6 men were observed working with pulley ropes hauling up full sandbags from supposed new dug out at A.29.b.1.3.

2. At 3.50pm. men observed working in trench at A.28.b.8.3 using mallet & stakes. They did not wear caps.

3. At 5.20pm. a man was observed looking over parapet at A.28.b.2.9. - he was fired on by our snipers & seen to fall - He was wearing a helmet which covered his ~~head~~ ears & back of his neck.

4. Nothing further to report this morning.

Lieut Col

19/7/16.

TACTICAL PROGRESS REPORT.

By O.C. 9th Seaforth Highlanders for 24 hours ended 4 A.M. 19th July 1916.

(To reach Brigade Headquarters by 8 A.M. daily.)

1. **HOSTILE ARTILLERY.** (a) Hostile artillery generally quiet during the period. RESERVE TRENCH was lightly shelled at 11.30pm yesterday & again at 4.30 am this morning.

Note. The following points to be supplied, wherever possible :-
(a) Time; (b) nature of projectile; (c) direction from which fired.

2. **TRENCH MORTARS.**
(a) <u>Our Action.</u> 114th L.M. Battery fired 52 rounds during the period. Target enemy front & support trenches about pts G.4.b.4.5½ & G.4.b.6½.6. In retaliation for enemy heavy trench mortars.

(b) <u>Enemy action.</u> Enemy were active with heavy trench mortars between 10.30pm & 11pm yesterday. STICKY TRENCH & NORTHAMPTON TRENCH between Bogan 110 & 112 - apparently from about pt G.4.b.3.9. Our artillery were informed. Enemy heavy trench mortars again active at 3.15 AM this morning from pt G.4.b.3.9. We replied with trench mortars - Artillery were also asked to retaliate.

3. **INFANTRY.** (Including Lewis guns, Machine guns, Rifle grenade and bomb operations, and patrolling.)

(a) <u>Our action.</u> During the period our Lewis Guns fired 1300 rounds, traversing enemy front & support line at G.4.b.6. A party of the enemy were heard working on their wire at pt G.4.b.3½.7. Fire was opened by our Lewis Guns & work ceased. A patrol went out from STICKY TRENCH at 11pm, enemy were heard working on their grappling - a small party was also heard working on enemy's wire & fired on by our Lewis Gun as above. Patrol returned at 3am. No hostile patrols encountered.
Our rifle grenade batteries were active on enemy sapheads - & our bombers were active with Hales Bomb from cup attachment.

(b) <u>Enemy action.</u>
Enemy not very active with rifle grenades.
Enemy snipers active during the night.

4. MISCELLANEOUS.   Mining, Air activity, etc.

It is believed that a relief has recently taken place on our front, since the afternoon of 16th inst. The enemy's behaviour has in many small ways been different; a man has shown himself opposite one of our saps, (near Russian Sap) & has made friendly signs to our men - this was before the attempted attack on our Sap head on night of 17th/18th. — Enemy snipers today are less active. Aerial darts are less frequent.

---

The activities of our Lewis and Machine guns and Trench Mortars should be given in a general way, stating total rounds expended for Machine guns and Stokes mortars roughly.
A list of each one of their targets is not required.

---

5. WIRING.   (i) New - giving approximate length and position.
(ii) Repair and strengthening of existing wire - giving position and length done.

Wiring of our Saps was continued by us.

---

(Sig.)_____

_____ 1916.

Note. In all reports the map references to points referred to should invariably be given.

TACTICAL PROGRESS REPORT.

By O.C. 8th Seaforth Highrs for 24 hours ending 12 Noon 20th July 1916

(To reach Brigade Headquarters by 8 A.M. daily.)

1. **HOSTILE ARTILLERY.**

Enemy artillery has been quiet on the whole. Northampton Trench between Boyau 110 & 112 was shelled at 9.45 p.m. yesterday for 15 minutes with 4.2's from direction of St ELIE little damage was done.

Enemy were again active between 8 a.m & 11 a.m. this morning with 4.2's on Northampton Trench between Boyau 109 & 111. Artillery retaliation was asked for.

Note. The following points to be supplied, whenever possible :-
(a) Time; (b) nature of projectile; (c) direction from which fired.

2. **TRENCH MORTARS.**

(a) Our Action.

Our light trench Mortars have fired 61 rounds during the period mainly on enemy's front line trench in retaliation for enemy aerial darts & trench Mortars - Our fire appeared in several cases to be quite accurate, & considerable damage was done to enemy trenches.

(b) Enemy action.

Enemy heavy trench Mortars active during the period - especially at 10.30pm when Stickly TRENCH was heavily shelled from about pt 65 A.4.2.9. They were again active at 8am this morning. Northampton Trench between Boyau 109 & 112 were heavily shelled. Artillery were informed on each occasion.

3. **INFANTRY.** (Including Lewis guns, Machine guns, Rifle grenade and bomb operations, and patrolling.)

(a) Our action.

(1) LEWIS GUNS. fired 1700 rounds traversing enemy front & support trenches. Many snipers who were active on top of crater about pt A.4.2.9. were fired on & snipers ceased.

(2) Listening patrols were out from Stickly Trench between 11pm & 3am. No signs of enemy working on his wire but enemy is still working on his front trench.

(3) Our bombers were active with rifle Grenades during the night on enemy Saphead.

(b) Enemy action.

Enemy were not very active with rifle grenades or aerial darts. Trench Mortars as reported in 2(b) very active.

T.O.

4. MISCELLANEOUS.   Mining, Air activity, etc.

1. At 3.30pm yesterday the enemy blew a mine at a point 50 yds NE of the NE end of Russian Saps in exactly the same place as the mine exploded by him on the night of 10/11th July. The Crater formed has enlarged the existing Crater, making it extend about 15 yds further West. No damage was done to our Sapheads or trenches. The situation remains unaltered.

2. At 5.30 a.m. this morning the enemy blew a small Camouflet about pt G.14.d.6.6. - Very little damage has been done to our trenches. One sniper plates on enemy's lip of Crater 2 were broken. Situation remains normal as before.

3. One sniper claims a hit on a German who exposed himself opposite No 4 Crater.

---

The activities of our Lewis and Machine guns and Trench Mortars should be given in a general way, stating total rounds expended for Machine guns and Stokes mortars roughly.
A list of each one of their targets is not required.

---

5. <u>WIRING.</u>   (i) New - giving approximate length and position.
(ii) Repair and strengthening of existing wire - giving position and length done.

The wiring of Russian Sap was continued with strengthening the existing wires.

---

(Sig.) _____ Lieut Col.
Cmdg Seaforth Hdrs.

20th July 1916.

Note. In all reports the map references to points referred to should invariably be given.

**XIV**

**TACTICAL PROGRESS REPORT.**

By O.C. 8th Seaforth Highlanders for 24 hours ende{ 12 noon. 21st July. 1916.
                                                   { 4 A.M.

(To reach Brigade Headquarters by 8 A.M. daily.)

1. **HOSTILE ARTILLERY.** Enemy artillery was quiet during the period. At 12.5 A.M. this morning the enemy sent up two red lights from the lip of Crater opposite ARGYLE SAP. This was immediately followed by about a dozen pip squeaks which fell close to the junction of Quarry Alley & Cannon Street.

Note. The following points to be supplied, whenever possible :-
   (a) Time; (b) nature of projectile; (c) direction from which fired.

2. **TRENCH MORTARS.**

   (a) Our Action. Our light mortars fired 67 rounds yesterday on enemy front & support trenches in G.4.b. On any occasion heavy firing, about 19 rounds from our light mortars silenced enemy heavy mortars.- The enemy's head at G.4.b.3½.8 was noticed to be badly damaged by our fire.

   (b) Enemy action. Enemy heavy mortars were active about 8.40 p.m. yesterday from pt G.4.b.3.9. Our retaliation with light mortars & heavy mortars was very quick & the enemy fire was silenced almost immediately.

3. **INFANTRY.** (Including Lewis guns, Machine guns, Rifle grenade and bomb operations, and patrolling.)

   (a) Our action. Lewis Guns fired 450 rounds traversing enemy front & support lines. A party of Germans working on their front line in G.4.b. was dispersed by our fire.
   Rifle Grenades. During the night we kept up a steady fire with Rifle grenades & bombs from cup attachment on enemy lips of craters. A working party at G.4.d.6.6. evidently repairing the damage done by enemy mine blown yesterday was fired on several times & dispersed.

   (b) Enemy action. Enemy snipers were very quiet during the period. Enemy replied to our rifle grenade fire with dart rifle grenades no damage was done.
   Enemy machine guns were active traversing our parapet & during the night the enemy kept throwing bombs into his own line.

T.O.

Patrols. Listening patrol went out between
11pm & 3am from Sticky Trench. Small enemy
party heard working on his wire - party dispersed
by our machine gun fire.
Enemy again heard working on his front line.

4. MISCELLANEOUS.    Mining, Air activity, etc.

It is believed that Enemy "observes"
for his trench mortars from his
Crater lips - (not always the same ones)

I think it is of great importance
that we get better
command of Enemy lips & craters.
For this Skilled labour is
required for construction of
loopholes, etc.
WW.

The activities of our Lewis and Machine guns and Trench Mortars
should be given in a general way, stating total rounds expended
for Machine guns and Stokes mortars roughly.
A list of each one of their targets is not required.

5. WIRING.    (i) New - giving approximate length and position.
              (ii) Repair and strengthening of existing wire -
                   giving position and length done.

Continued round Sap head
North of Russian Sap.

21/7/16 1916.    (Sig.) _____
                        Capt. & Adjutant

Note. In all reports the map references to points referred to
should invariably be given.

**SECRET**
**URGENT.**

**XV**

All Recipients of O.O. No. 4 dated July 21st 1916:—

Ref. O.O. No. 4 d/July 21st 1916, the Battalion will move to Billets in NOEUX-LES-MINES, to-morrow, and not VERQUIN. as previously ordered.

July 21st 1916

G.W. Duncan Lieut. & Adjutant
8th Battn. Seaforth Highlanders.

Operation Order No 4
by
Lieut. Col. N. A. Thomson D.S.O.
Commdg 8th Battn Seaforth Highlanders
July 21st 1916

Copy No 8.

1. The 8th Battn Seaforth Highlanders will be relieved by the 2nd Battn Rifle Brigade in the Left Subsection, HOHENZOLLERN SECTION tomorrow 22nd July 1916.

2. Companies will be relieved in the following order:—

   "C" Company 8th Seaforth Highrs by "C" Company 2nd Rifle Brigade.
   "D" Company        do        do    by "B" Company        do        do.
   "A" Company        do        do    by "A" Company        do        do.
   "B" Company        do        do    by "D" Company        do        do.

   Lewis Guns will be relieved with their Companies.—

   Guides:— 1 per platoon & 1 per Lewis Gun, & 1 for Headquarters will be at CLARKE'S KEEP at 9-15 a.m. tomorrow to guide incoming Companies of 2nd Rifle Brigade.

   Route for incoming Companies:— QUARRY ALLEY & NORTHAMPTON TRENCH.

   On relief Companies of 8th Seaforth Highrs will move to VERQUIN, via BART'S ALLEY, VERMELLES, CROSS ROADS, PHILOSOPHE, CROSS ROADS in L.17.b. CROSS ROADS in L.17.c. & thence via RED ROAD to NOEUX-LES-MINES and from NOEUX-LES-MINES to VERQUIN via Main NOEUX - BETHUNE ROAD.

   All movements East of NOEL to be by platoons at 300 yards interval.

3. O.C. Companies concerned will hand over any listening galleries in their area to the incoming Companies.

4. O.C. "B" Coy will detail an officer to remain at BREWERY, VERMELLES to take charge of the permanent carrying party at present working with Tunnelling Companies & march them to VERQUIN on relief.

5. Advanced parties of 2nd Rifle Brigade consisting of 1 officer per battalion and 1 N.C.O per Company to take over trench stores will be at CLARKE'S KEEP at 7-15 a.m. tomorrow where they will be met by one guide per Company & 1 from Headquarters.

   Receipts for all Trench Stores will be taken & sent to Battn Headquarters by 6 p.m. 23rd July.

6. The No 1 of each Lewis gun of 8th Seaforth Highrs will remain with incoming team until their services can be dispensed with, when they will rejoin the Battalion in billets.

7. All dixchies and remaining mess kit will be brought down to CLARKE'S KEEP by 8 a.m. tomorrow.

   The Transport Officer will detail ½ a limber per Company and 1 limber for Headquarters to be at CLARKE'S KEEP at 8 a.m. to transport this baggage to VERQUIN.

8. First Line Transport will move from SAILLY LABOURSE to VERQUIN via NOEUX-LES-MINES under arrangements to be made by the Transport Officer.

9. All trenches, latrines etc. will be left scrupulously clean and a certificate obtained from the incoming company Commanders that their condition is satisfactory.

10. Completion of relief will be reported to Battalion Headquarters and O.C. Companies will report as soon as their Company is in billets.

George W. Duncan.
Lieutenant.
Adjt. 8th Battn Seaforth Highlanders.

Distribution:—  Copy No 1. O.C. "A" Coy.      No 6. Transport Officer.
                     No 2. O.C. "B" Coy.      No 7. O.C. 2nd Battn Rifle Brigade.
                     No 3. O.C. "C" Coy.      No 8. War Diary.
                     No 4. O.C. "D" Coy.      No 9. File.
                     No 5. Lewis Gun Officer.

SECRET

**Operation Order No 5**
by
Lieut. Col. N. A. Thomson D.S.O.
Commdg. 8th Battn. Seaforth Highrs
July 22nd 1916

Copy No. 9

XVI

1. Reference 1/40000 Map. - Sheet 36.B.

2. The Battalion will march tomorrow as under:-
   Starting Point :- CROSS ROADS K.18.b.7.0.
   Time :- 8.0. a.m.
   Order of March :- "A", "B", "C", "D" Coys, Lewis Gun Detachment.
   Route :- FORKED ROAD, Pt K.18.C.1.4½, Cross Roads K.15.C.3.8, HALLICOURT, BRUAY STATION (Pt J.16.d) DIVION & thence to OURTON.

3. Billeting Party of 1 N.C.O. per Coy & 1 for Headquarters under 2/Lieut. J.H. Ross will pass Pt. K.18.C.1.4 at 8.24 a.m. & march in rear of Brigade Headquarters as far as BRUAY STATION when they will go forward with STAFF CAPTAIN. This party will be mounted on bicycles to be drawn from Signal Station.

4. Echelon "A" of 1st Line Transport will march in rear of the Battalion. Echelon "B" will march under Brigade Transport Officer, and will pass Pt K.15.C.3.8 at 9.25 a.m.

5. Dress will be full marching order. Shrapnel Helmets will be worn strapped on to the Pack.

6. Officers valises will be taken to Quartermasters Stores by 7 a.m. - mess boxes will be collected at 7.30 a.m.

7. Refilling Point for 23rd July - BETHUNE-VERQUIN ROAD 10. a.m.

George W. Duncan
Lieutenant.
Adjt. 8th Battn. Seaforth Highlanders.

Copy. No 1. - O.C. "A" Coy.         No 6 - Transport Officer.
      2. - O.C. "B" Coy.             7 - 2nd Lieut. J.H. Ross.
      3. - O.C. "C" Coy.             8 - War Diary.
      4. - O.C. "D" Coy.             9 - File.
      5. - Lewis Gun Officer.       10 -

March Table to accompany 44th Infantry Brigade Operation Order No.87, dated 22-7-16.

| UNITS. | STARTING POINT. | | TIME. A.M. | ROUTE. | DESTINATION. | REMARKS. |
|---|---|---|---|---|---|---|
| In order of march. | PLACE. | | | | | |
| 44th Inf.Bde. H.Q. and Bde.Sig.Secn: | Cross Roads. Pt.K.15.c.3.8. | | 9-0 | HAILLICOURT (Pt.J.16.d) - BRUAY STN. - DIVION. | DIEVAL. | To clear subsidiary Starting Point, Forked Road Pt.K.18. c.1.4. at 8-24 A.M. |
| 9th Black Watch. | As above. | | 9-1 | As above to DIVION, thence via OURTON - DIEVAL. | LA THIEULOYE. | |
| 7th Cameron Hrs. | As above. | | 9-6 | As above. | DIEVAL. | |
| 8/10th Gordon Hrs. | As above. | | 9-11 | As above. | DIEVAL. | To pass above Starting Point at 8-25 A.M. |
| 8th Seaforth Hrs. | As above. | | 9-16 | As above - as far as OURTON. | OURTON. | To pass above Starting Point at 8-30 A.M. |
| 44th T.M.Battery. | As above. | | 9-21 | As above - as far as DIEVAL. | DIEVAL. | To pass above Starting Point at 8-35 A.M. |
| 44th M.G.Coy. | As above. | | 9-22 | As above - as far as DIEVAL. | DIEVAL. | To pass above Starting Point at 8-36 A.M. |
| Brigadod 1st Line Transport, Echelon "B". | As above. | | 9-25 | As above to OURTON and thence by same route as units to which portions belong. | Billets of units. | Portion belonging to Units from NOEUX to follow 44th M.G.Coy. |
| 46th Fld.Amb. | BRUAY STN. Pt.J.16.d. | | 10-45 | DIVION. | OURTON. | Via road S.of Railway from RUITZ to Rly. |
| No.2 Coy.Train. | Cross Roads. Pt.K.15.c.3.8. | | After re-filling. | As for Brigade H.Qrs. | DIEVAL. | |

Headquarters Mess.
O.C. All Companies.
Lewis Gun Officer.
Transport Officer.
Medical Officer.

**XVII**

HEADQUARTERS.
Date
No.
8th. (S) Battn. Seaforth Highrs.

## TRAINING

1. The Battn. less Transport will march out tomorrow as under:-

   STARTING POINT — Forked Roads at I.34.b.5.6.
   TIME — 9-30 a.m.
   ORDER OF MARCH — "B" "C" "D" "A" Coys, Lewis Gun Detatchment.
   ROUTE — Main Road from OURTON to DIÉVAL
   DRESS — Full Marching Order. (O.C. Companies are reminded that the steel helmets are to be carried on the pack underneath the pack straps).

2. This will be a muster parade, the only exceptions being
   Company Cooks.
   2 Officers Servants per Company.

3. O.C. Companies will forward to Battn Headquarters by 8 a.m. tomorrow a list of any men to be left behind, for any reason whatever.

4. 2/Lieut. F.W. Ashard will attend.

5. All men unable to march will parade under 2/Lieutenant W.M. Potter outside Battn Orderly Room at 9-15 a.m. 2/Lieut Potter will report to the Adjutant for instructions.

6. Sick Parade will be at 7 a.m.

George W. Duncan Lieutenant.
Adj. 8th Battn Seaforth Highrs

24-7-16

Head Quarters Tues

## OPERATION ORDER No. XVIII No. 9
by
Lieut. Col. N. A. Thomson, D.S.O.
Commdg. 8th (S) Battn. Seaforth Highlanders — July 25th 1916

1. The Battalion will march to new billets to-morrow as under:-
   STARTING POINT :- Forked Roads just S. of OURTON BRIDGE.
   TIME :- 6-30 a.m.
   ORDER OF MARCH :- "C", "D", "A" and "B" Coys; Lewis Gun
   Detatchment; 1st Line Transport (Echelon A.)

2. Billeting party of 1 N.C.O per Coy. and 1 for Headquarters will parade outside Battalion H.Q. under 2/Lieut. J.H. Ross at 6 a.m. to-morrow. — Special instructions will be issued to 2/Lieut. J.H. Ross.

3. Echelon "B", 1st Line Transport, will follow the Battalion. Baggage waggons will accompany Echelon "B".

4. Officer's Valises will be taken to Quartermaster's stores by 5.45 a.m - Mess boxes will be collected at 6 a.m.

5. Refilling point to-morrow on BRYAS-DIEVAL ROAD just N.E of BRYAS.......... Time 11 a.m.

DISTRIBUTION
Copy No 1. O.C "A" Coy.
    2. O.C "B" Coy.
    3. O.C "C" Coy.
    4. O.C "D" Coy.
    5. Lewis Gun Officer
    6. Transport officer.
    7. 2/Lt. J.H. Ross
    8. Headquarters Mess
    9. War Diary
    10. File

George W. Duncan
Lieut.
Adjutant 8th Seaforth Highlanders

March Table to accompany 44th Infantry Brigade Operation Order No.68, dated 25-7-16.

| UNITS. In order of march. | STARTING PLACE. | POINT. TIME. A.M. | ROUTE. | DESTINATION. | REMARKS. |
|---|---|---|---|---|---|
| 44th Bde.H.Q. and Bde. Signal Section. | Southern end of | 8-0 | MONCHY BRETON - BAILLEUL aux-CORNAILLES. | MAIRIE, AVERDOINGT. | To move to starting point via X Roads immediately S. of A of ANTIGNEUL CHATEAU. |
| 9th Black Watch. | LA THIEULOYE | 8-1 | As above. | MAGNICOURT-sur-CANCHE. | |
| 44th M.G.Coy. | at road | 8-6 | As above. | AVERDOINGT. | To clear road immediately on arrival for remainder of column. |
| 7th Cameron Hrs. | junction on | 8-9 | As above. | GOUY-en-TERNOIS. | To march to starting point by same road as Brigade H.Qrs. |
| 8/10th Gordon Hrs. | the more | 8-14 | As above. | MAIZIERES. | As above. |
| 44th T.M.Battery. | westerly of | 8-19 | As above. | AVERDOINGT. | On arrival at destination to clear the road. |
| 91st Fld.Coy.R.E. | the two roads to | 8-20 | As above. | GOUY-en-TERNOIS. | As above. |
| 8th Seaforth Hrs. Echelon "B". Brigaded 1st Line Transport. | MONCHY - BRETON. | 8-24 8-29 | As above. As above. | AVERDOINGT. Billets of Units. | To move to starting point by DIEVAL, and thence by same road as Bde.H.Qrs. |
| 46th Fld.Amb. | | 8-39 | As above. | MAIZIERES. | As for 8th Seaforth Hrs. |

Copy No. 109

## ~ OPERATION ORDER No 7 ~

Lieut.Col N. A. Thomson, D.S.O,
~ Commdg 8th (S) Battalion Seaforth Highlanders ~ July 26th 1916.

Reference Map - LENS SHEET - 1/100,000.

**XIX**

1. The Battalion will march to new billets as under:-
   - STARTING POINT — Cross Roads just north of the A.V. in AVENDOINGT
   - TIME — 7.5 a.m.
   - ORDER OF MARCH — "D", "A", "B" and "C" Coys., Lewis Gun Detachment, 1st Line Transport (Echelon A.)

---

2. Echelon "B", 1st Line Transport, including baggage waggons will follow the Battalion.

---

3. Billeting party (on bicycles) of 1 N.C.O per Coy. and 1 for Headquarters, will parade at 6.30 a.m. to-morrow, outside Battn. H.Q, under 2/Lieut. J.H. Ross - special instructions will be issued to 2/Lieut. J.H. Ross.

---

4. Officers' Valises will be taken to Quartermasters Stores by 6.15 a.m. Mess Boxes will be collected at 6.30 a.m.

---

5. Refilling point on 27th July will be notified later.

---

................................... Lieut.
Adjutant, 8th Seaforth Highlanders.

Distribution    Copy No. 1  O.C "A" Coy
                       2  O.C "B" Coy
                       3  O.C "C" Coy
                       4  O.C "D" Coy
                       5  Lewis Gun officer
                       6  Transport officer
                       7  2/Lieut. J.H. Ross
                       8  Headquarters Mess
                       9  War Diary
                      10  File.

March Table to accompany 44th Infantry Brigade Operation Order No.69, dated 26/7/16.

| UNITS. In order of march. | STARTING POINT. PLACE. | TIME. A.M. | ROUTE. | DESTINATION. | REMARKS. |
|---|---|---|---|---|---|
| 44th Bde.H.Q. and Bde.Signal Section. | Western exit from MAGNICOURT-sur-CANCHE. | 8-0 | HOUVIN - | OCCOCHES. | To move to starting point via GOUAY-en-TERNOIS. |
| 9th Black Watch. | | 8-1 | HOUVIGNEUL - | OCCOCHES. | |
| 7th Cameron Hrs. | | 8-6 | HONVAL - | OCCOCHES. | |
| 91st Fld.Coy.R.E. | | 8-11 | REBREUVE - | REMAISNIL. | To move to starting point via GOUAY-en-TERNOIS. |
| 44th M.G.Coy. | | 8-15 | CANTELEUX. | REMAISNIL. | |
| 44th L.M.Battery. | | 8-18 | | REMAISNIL. | As above. |
| 8/10th Gordon Hrs. | | 8-19 | | BARLY. | To move to starting point via GOUAY-en-TERNOIS. |
| 8th Seaforth Hrs. Brigaded 1st Line Transport. Echelon "B". | | 8-24 8-29 | | BARLY. Billets of Units. | |
| 46th Fld.Amb. | | 8-39 | | BARLY. | |

– Operation Order No 8 –    Copy No. 19

– Lieut Col. N. A. Thomson D.S.O. –
Commanding 8th Battn Seaforth Highlanders
27th July 1916

XX

Reference Map.
   LENS Sheet 1/10000

1. The Battalion will march to new billets tomorrow as under:—
    Starting Point – Forked Roads immediately N.W. of the "B" in BARLY.
    Time – 7-30 a.m.
    Order of March – "A", "B", "C", "D" Coys, Lewis Gun Detatchment, 1st Line Transport (Echelon "A")

2. Echelon "B" 1st Line Transport will follow the battalion.

3. Billeting Party of 1 N.C.O. per Coy and 1 for Headquarters will parade outside Battalion Headquarters at 6-30 a.m. tomorrow under 2/Lieut. J. N. Ross. — Special instructions will be issued to him.

4. Officers Valises will be taken to Quartermasters Stores by 6-45 a.m. Mess boxes will be collected at 7 a.m.

5. Refilling Point for 28th July will be notified later.

                      George W. Sim
                                  Lieutenant.
             Adjutant 8th Battalion Seaforth Highrs.

Copy No. 1  O.C. "A" Coy.     Copy No. 6. Transport Officer.
       2  O.C. "B" Coy.           7  2/Lieut. J.N.Ross.
       3  O.C. "C" Coy.           8  Hqrs. Res.
       4  O.C. "D" Coy.           9  War Diary.
       5  Lewis Gun Officer.    10  File.

All recipients of Operation Order No 8 issued 27-7-16.

Note see about operation orders.

1/ Head of the column will pass the starting point at 7-5 a.m. instead of 7-30 a.m.

2. Billeting party will parade at 6-0 a.m. and not 6-30 a.m.

3. Officers Valises will be at Q.M. Stores by 6-15 a.m. and mess types will be collected at 6-30 a.m.

27-7-16

C.P. M'Iver
Capt. 6th Bn of the Cameronians

Casualties for July 1916

July 1 1 man Wounded & Died at Divl School at GOSNAY
2 Nil
3 Nil
4 Nil
5 Nil
6 1 Off Wounded at NOYELLES (Lt Morocco S.J.)
7 1 man Wounded
8 1 man Wounded
9 3 men Wounded
10 1 man Killed
10/1 6 offs & 74 men Wounded 9 men Killed
11 2 men Wounded & 1 Off & 1 man Killed
12 1 man Wounded
13 1 man Wounded
14 4 men Wounded 1 man Killed
15 9 men Wounded & 2 men Killed
16 3 men Wounded & 4 men Killed
17 3 men Wounded & 1 man Killed
18 2 men Wounded & 1 Off Wounded
19 2 men Wounded 1 man Killed
20 6 men Wounded
21 3 men Wounded
22 1 man Wounded & 1 man Killed

No Casualties after this date

P.T.O.

## Names of Officers

| | | |
|---|---|---|
| July 6th | Lieut S. J. Morrell | Wounded |
| July 10/11 { | Capt L Holmes | } Wounded |
| | Capt D.O. Hart | |
| | Lieut J.E. Smith | |
| | 2/Lieut J.M. McCallum | |
| | 2/Lieut A.J.M. Miller | |
| | 2/Lieut K. MacKenzie | |
| July 11 | 2/Lieut J.M.E. Nicholson | Killed |
| July 18 | 2/Lieut H.J. Kirkpatrick | Wounded |

S E C R E T.           XXIII

44th Brigade B.M.667.

WARNING ORDER.

The Brigade will probably move from its present area on 2nd August.

Issued to recipients of
44th Brigade O.O.No.70.
31-7-16.

LaBeck.
Major,
Brigade Major,
44th Infantry Brigade.

of Officers Casualties
for July. 1916.

July 6th. Lieutenant. S. J. Morrell. Wounded

July 10/1 {
Capt. F Holmes
Capt. J.G. Hart.
Lieut. J.E Smith
2/Lieut. F.M. McCallion
2/Lieut. A.J.M. Miller.
2/Lieut. K. MacKenzie.
} Wounded.

July 11th 2/Lieut. J.McL. Nicholson — Killed.

July 18th. 2/Lieut. H.J. Kirkpatrick Wounded

March Table to accompany 44th Infantry Brigade Operation Order No.70,
dated 30-7-16.

| UNITS. In order of march. | STARTING POINT. Place. | Time. A.M. | ROUTE. | DESTINATION. | REMARKS. |
|---|---|---|---|---|---|
| 44th Inf.Bde.H.Q. & Sig.Secn: | The | 6-30 | The | NAOURS. | |
| 8th Seaforth Hrs. | | 6-32 | | NAOURS. | |
| 44th M.G.Coy. | Church | 6-39 | most | WARGNIES. | |
| 44th T.M.Battery. | VALHEUREUX | 6-43 | direct | WARGNIES. | |
| 91st Fld.Coy.R.E. | | 6-46 | | WARGNIES. | |
| 8/10th Gordon Hrs. | | 6-50 | route. | NAOURS. | |
| 46th Fld.Amb. | | 6-57 | | WARGNIES. | To drop 2 ambulances which will follow in rear of column from Starting Point. |
| 9th Black Watch. | | 7-2 | | NAOURS. | |
| 7th Cameron Hrs. | | 7-9 | | NAOURS. | |

Units from AUTHEUX and LONGUEVILLETTE will move to starting point
    CANDAS.

Units from GEZAINCOURT will move to starting point via road passing
    between V and second A of BEAUVAL.

S E C R E T.

All Units 44th Inf.Bde.
  91st R.E.
  No.2 Coy.Train.

44th Brigade B.M.648.
15th Div. No.1393 G.S.

XXI

    The whole Division will probably march to VIGNACOURT Area on 31st instant.  The proposal to move Infantry by train is cancelled.

                         E.a.Beck
                              Major,
                          Brigade Major,
29-7-16.              44th Infantry Brigade.

# OPERATION ORDER No 9.

Lieut. Col. N. A. Thomson, D.S.O,
by
Comndg. 8th (S) Battn. Seaforth Highrs.   July 3rd 1916

Reference Map.  LENS SHEET 1/100,000:

**XXII**

1. The Battalion will march to new Billets to-morrow as under:-

   STARTING POINT — Cross Roads ½ mile S.E. of "x" in BAGNEUX.
   TIME ............. — 4·30 a.m.
   ORDER of MARCH — "B" "C" "D" & "A" Coys, Lewis Gun Detachment, 1st line Transport (Echelon "A" + "B")

2. Billeting party of 1 N.C.O. per Coy. and 1 for Headquarters will parade outside Battalion H.Q. at 4·15 a.m. to-morrow under 2/Lieut. J. H. Ross — special instructions will be issued to him. This party will be mounted on bicycles.

3. Officers Valises will be taken to Quartermasters Stores by 3·45 a.m. Mess boxes will be collected at 4 a.m.

4. Reveillé will be at 2·30 a.m. to-morrow.
   Sick Parade at 3 a.m.

5. Refilling point on 31st July will be notified later.

George W. Duncan.
Capt.,
Adjutant, 8th Bn. Seaforth Highrs

DISTRIBUTION

Copy. No 1. O.C "A" Coy.
        2. O.C "B" Coy.
        3. O.C "C" Coy.
        4. O.C "D" Coy
        5. Lewis Gun Officer
        6. Transport Officer
        7. 2/Lieut. J. H. Ross.
        8. Headquarters Mess.
        9. War Diary
        10. File.

SECRET.  44th Brigade B.M.634.

Addressed recipients of 44th Brigade
Operation Order No.69.

WARNING ORDER for 28-7-16.

1. The Starting Point will be Road Junction ½ mile South East of S in OUTREBOIS, at 8 A.M.

2. Order of march as for to-day.

3. Route and billets will be notified later.

4. It is not expected that the march will be more than 4 or 5 miles.

                        Major,
                     Brigade Major,
27-7-16.              44th Infantry Brigade.

March Table to accompany 44th Infantry Brigade B.M.635.

| UNIT. In order of march. | STARTING POINT. PLACE. | TIME. A.M. | ROUTE. | DESTINATION. |
|---|---|---|---|---|
| 44 Bde.H.Qrs.& Sig.Secn: | Cross Roads | 7-44 | BY | AUTHEUX. |
| 9th Black Watch. | immediately | 7-45 | most | LONGUEVILLETTE. |
| 7th Cameron Hrs. | West of | 7-51 | direct | AUTHEUX. |
| 8/10th Gordon Hrs. | O of | 7-57 | route. | GEZAINCOURT. |
| 8th Seaforth Hrs. | OCCOCHES. | 8-3 | | - do - |
| 44th M.G.Coy. | | 8-9 | | - do - |
| 44th T.M.Battery. | | 8-12 | | - do - |
| 91st Fld.Coy.R.E. | | 8-13 | | - do - |
| 46th Fld.Amb. | | 8-17 | | - do - |

REMARKS.
1st Line Transport, Echelons "A" and "B" and baggage wagons, will accompany units.

No.2 Coy.Train will billet at GEZAINCOURT.

S E C R E T.                                44th Brigade B.M.635.

1. This office No.B.M.634 of to-day's date is cancelled.

2. Units will march to billets on 28th instant in accordance with attached march table.

3. Billeting parties at starting point at 6-30 A.M.

4. Brigade Headquarters will close at OCCOCHES at 8 A.M. and re-open at MAIRIE, AUTHEUX.

5. Refilling Point to-morrow on AUXI-le-CHATEAU – DOULLENS Road immediately N.W. of FROHEN-le-GRAND, at 11 A.M.

27-7-16.

Issued to all
 Recipients of 44th
 Inf.Bde. O.O. No.69.

Major,
Brigade Major,
44th Infantry Brigade.

www.ingramcontent.com/pod-product-compliance
Lightning Source LLC
Chambersburg PA
CBHW081422160426
43193CB00013B/2169